Coin of Brokenness

Which Side of Brokenness Are You?

MARK E. FULTZ

ISBN 979-8-88685-472-5 (paperback)
ISBN 979-8-88685-473-2 (digital)

Christian Faith Publishing
832 Park Avenue
Meadville, PA 16335
www.christianfaithpublishing.com

Printed in the United States of America

I would like to dedicate this book, *Coin of Brokenness*, to my precious family. Thank you for being so patient with me.

My wife, Laura:

My childhood sweetie, my teenage crush, my lifelong companion, my friend, supporter, and partner in ministry. Sweetheart, I love you more than life itself. You bring me so much fulfillment. You are the best!

My boys, Daryl and Robert:

Proud of my US Marines. Your love and support is so encouraging.

My daughter, Nevaeh:

You truly are a gift from Heaven. Love you so much. Thanks for loving your dad.

My daughters-in-law, Karissa and Lottie:

You're just like my own kiddos. Thanks for loving my boys. I love you both more than I can say.

My grands! Brecker and Brielynn:

You are my treasures for sure! This Papa loves you both immensely.

Two treasures in Heaven: Sheryl Marie and a Grand!

Contents

Preface

We reference that it takes two to have an argument, or there are two sides to every story. We also know there are two sides to every coin. We think of it as heads and tails. Most sporting events have the coin toss in which certain starting benefits are determined. A choice is called before the coin is tossed. It is a fifty-fifty chance you will get your wish. It could go either direction. You have to be prepared to advance according to the results. Will it be an offensive attack, or will it be a defensive stand?

Brokenness is not a choice you would make. It is not a goal you would set out to achieve. Unfortunately, it happens. How we process brokenness is what's important. There are two sides to brokenness. One side is the traumatic experience that is disabling—an event or circumstances that disrupts your ability to process life in a normal or reasonable fashion. The other side of brokenness is the triumph of the recovery—the process which enables you to find the healthy acceptance or response. Each moment that brokenness may occur, there will be some kind of response. We may think of it as either positive or negative. The mystery is that not all traumatic experiences are equal. Even though individuals may encounter similar circumstances, it does not mean the reactions will be identical. There usually is some other backstory that deeply influences the particular response. Brokenness does not have to be your handicap; it can be your asset.

God put a call upon my life at the young age of twelve to be a Minister of His Gospel. I have been in Pastoral Ministry approaching thirty years. Those years have put many people into my life. I have listened to multiple accounts of serious woes and horrifying tales of brokenness. I have wept with those troubled souls. The accounts related to me are just a mere sampling to the plethora of traumatic experiences I have witnessed. Lives and families have been torn apart by tragedy. Brokenness has divided marriages and separated children. With tears streaming down countless cheeks, I have listened to the torments people were suffering. My office has been their podium to tell their story. Ministry has given me the opportunity to be an active participant in the role as a first responder. Being a firefighter and emergency medical responder has put me at the scene of many individuals in their critical, traumatic experience. As a leading member of the Critical Incident Stress Management Team, I have heard countless stories of trauma and its debilitating impact on their person. The struggles of first responders are serious and have led many to despair and the choice to end life. The reality of brokenness is a real, true-life story.

There is a personal side to this unique *Coin of Brokenness*. I have carried many coins. My pockets have been heavy with them. As I deposited these coins into the bank of God's grace, another coin was handed to me, and into my pocket it would go. No matter how I wished to forget about these weights, they would come crashing from my grasp to the ground at my feet. The noise from these dropping coins would cascade through my dome of human connections. I would be so humiliated by this display of brokenness erupting from my innermost being. No matter how hard I would try to fix it, overcome the hurts, or make honest amends, I still was broken. There came a turning point in this journey that set my feet in a healthy direction. I embraced my brokenness. God had a different agenda for me than what I had imagined. It was time to see what God was going to do.

My story is not something special that is superior to your story. I share some portraits of my story along with some insights I have learned, so that maybe I can inspire and encourage you. Brokenness is not pleasant, but it can be profitable. It makes all the difference in how you approach the events of your life as to how it personally impacts you. All your life's choices and decisions are invariably linked to elements of brokenness. It can also be seen that our decision-making repeats the storyline of brokenness. Now is the time to stop the repeated cycle and find the beauty of a living redemption.

Introduction

Why talk about broken things? No one deliberately seeks to secure an item that is incomplete or fractured. I recognize that there are individuals who find reward in procuring those relics that are less than perfect. They will invest themselves into recreating or restoring its condition to reflect the original as close as possible. Others embark on repurposing these items from previous generations of use into a new fashion which are then displayed in an attractive manner.

So why take something from a material dimension and explore an application into the psychology of thought and identity? Is there a spiritual component to brokenness? Brokenness is a part of life. We cannot escape its harsh reality. There is no person, institution, or setting that is exempt from the experiences of being broken. Many would rather ignore the fact or flee from any reference to being broken than face the humiliating repercussions for admitting its presence. The stigma, the shunning, the staring gaze become painful needles to the heart and mind that has already been wounded. Denial becomes the reaction, and we passionately defend our positions.

Without any recognition of brokenness in your own life, it will be very difficult to begin to understand what might be evident to you in the life of another person. A potential negative in sharing on the subject of brokenness is for someone to get the impression that it now becomes their responsibility to find brokenness in other people. The focus is not for one to inspect others, but to see the brokenness in your own life and to grow from it. There is nothing lonelier than to feel that no one understands or can see your pain.

The words upon these pages are for you, the one you see in the mirror every morning and wish someone would just take a few moments of time to sit in your life's corner. This resource is for you, the one who lies awake night after night, staring into the darkness, just wishing and hoping for some caring soul to lend a listening ear and loving heart. The darkness of your soul and spirit which engulfs the broken needs the light of hope. Where can we find hope? Is hope even to be found? If you are the one who has encountered the injury that took you out of the game, the game is not over. If you sense that you are stuck on the side of road watching others pass you by, help is on the way. The line of individuals fighting the demons of depression from brokenness is long. However, your story is not over—neither is your last chapter written. Yes, the brokenness of life is real, but there is hope. Someone does care, and He is already calling your name. Can you hear Him? Help is on the way. As the hand of help is being extended, go ahead and extend your hand. The lift is rewarding. There is a new day before you needing your exploration. There is someone else that is needing you, and you might be the only person to make that intimate connection. I share with you that brokenness isn't final. Brokenness can be the stepping stones to tell a beautiful story.

There is healing and hope from every detail of brokenness. The healing may not remove the scars, but it changes our focus into a new direction. It looks beyond the environment around us and seeks to find a new normal from the rubble of brokenness. Hope is not determined by our brokenness; in spite of being broken, we rise again and look beyond ourselves for meaning and purpose.

Yes, talk about your brokenness, but make sure you talk about your healing.

PART ONE

The Trauma of Brokenness

Defining Brokenness

Have you ever had the hiccups? Brokenness is like having the hiccups. It is both annoying and frustrating. You didn't do anything to start them, and even though well-intentioned remedies are offered, there is really nothing you can do to stop them. You eventually come to the awareness that they are gone. You function in spite of hiccupping. It is the duration of having the hiccups that sets a parameter of considering what I am labeling brokenness. Everyone has had hiccups of all variations in their lifetime. Some parameters of brokenness are short-lived, while other parameters are permanent.

Let's define brokenness a bit more closely rather than a haphazard hiccup.

> Individual trauma results from an event, series of events, or set of circumstances that is experienced by an individual as physically or emotionally harmful or life threatening and that has lasting adverse effects on the individual's functioning and mental, physical, social, emotional,

or spiritual well-being. (Substance and Mental Health Services Adm. 2014, PA Dept of Health)

Simply put, brokenness is the result of some form of a traumatic experience. Who really can say who does or does not have brokenness for some form of traumatic event? It is only the person who has experienced it. No one else has any authority to deem it non-traumatic. Experiences are interpreted by the person's perception. It may be an incorrect interpretation, but the perception is what inflicts the element of the struggle of brokenness. We might consider items such as war, physical abuse, sudden death, accidents, etc. as being Big T (traumatic) items. Other significant items such as bullying, verbal assaults, failures, rejections, etc. may be labeled as Little T. However, the brokenness that follows any type of these kind of traumatic experiences is the same. It becomes the major hiccup in trying to process life. It is the inhibitor to healthy thought processes. It becomes the foundation to many formed negative behaviors. Once any form of brokenness occurs, it deeply affects any other traumatic events that enters one's life. In fact, the response that develops is often exaggerated or magnified because of the accumulative effect or unresolved issues from the past. Failure to process these kinds of traumatic events in a healthy manner creates a vacuum that leaves unfulfilled purpose. A person's wholeness is lost, and the brokenness becomes an inhibiting reality.

There is no aspect of our human life that is completely perfect. There are happy homes and strong marriages, but the individuals within those beautiful relationships will have events which alter the picturesque setting. Have you ever had to apologize? Why? Was it the words you spoke, or how you spoke them? Maybe it was some other aspect of personal negligence that needed to be rectified. Even though there was not an intentional or deliberate choice to illicit pain or hurt, it happens. It may not be a single event that produces the element of brokenness, but it could be the repetitiveness of a particular action that eventually breaks the spirit of an individual. During one's lifetime, there is no way of knowing how many incidents of trauma may occur; just know they will.

God is constantly working redemptively in our lives. His redemptive reach is not only the persuasive power of His perfect love; He also allows difficulties into our lives for specific reasons. There are moments when the bottom falls away, and we are left with ashes and destroyed plans. Why would God allow this? It could be because we have never allowed Him into our lives, and the only way He could reveal Himself to us was to allow these reverses and setbacks. If we can quiet our outburst long enough, we just might hear His voice. When a trauma is experienced, God is always there. We may not feel it or sense Him close, but He is right beside us. We just aren't looking to Him readily. He knows what has happened against us. He does not condone any form of wickedness, but He is present to bring a story out of our distress that speaks of His greatness. Never overlook the face of God. You will not find His face in the eyes or voice of your accuser or abuser, but you will find His redemptive face lifting you up and guiding you through your brokenness to a story of His grace.

> ### *God is constantly working redemptively in our lives. Never overlook the face of God.*

I grew up in a wonderful home. It would be known as a Christian home. My parents both loved God and tried to rear us children to love God too. We were faithful, regular attendees of church. We were active in participating in church life. I was privileged to attend a wonderful Christian school and college. I guess you could say I had a "perfect" childhood. However, there were multiple scenarios that were presented to us that shattered this perceived image of perfection. These situations were so intense that I can remember them vividly even though they are over forty years in my past. It's like they are scars upon the film of memory. Some linger and still present themselves while other instances have become stepping stones on the triumphant path of healing and wholeness.

I thank God for my heritage. I am blessed indeed. There really are no complaints; just a new understanding of what human imperfection truly is. My parents were not perfect. Love overlooks a lot of imperfection. As I child, I never thought of them in any way but perfect. Yes, my family had its flaws. I was probably the poster child of imperfection; however, I somehow learned that to be accepted and loved, I had to be perfect. I had to do it just right. It was the affirmation this child needed. Anything less than perfect brought other emotional challenges that left me at different times inwardly broken. Add upon this increasing burden the strict, conservative standard of spirituality. To me, I learned that God would not accept me if I did not perform this conservative discipline well. Truthfully, in my mind, God was waiting to judge me severely if I would fail.

What this creates is a performance-based perspective. It would be the syllabus I would carry with me into my early years of ministry. It was my litmus test. It would also be the very reason I experienced one of the most difficult, low experiences of life. How can a broken person who could not live up to perfection overcome this crushing burden of failure? It happened, but from the broken shards of serious negativity and shattered worth came a new individual. I learned who God really was and not what I had made Him to be. I had a new awareness of the graciousness of God. I learned a deeper meaning to love that went beyond how well I performed. A dear friend pulled me aside during this breaking point and period of darkness and said a simple but profound statement. "God's grace is bigger than this." I found it to be true. Could it really be true that God was on my side and not "fighting" against me? This ray of hope began a new journey that continues to grow substantially to this day.

The performance trap was a big deal in my mind. I did not realize how negatively it impacted me personally and even my ministry. I had set a bar so high that it was virtually impossible to ever reach the goal. In turn, I demanded a lot from many people and judged them by the standard I had and tried to make it theirs. It did not go too well. Coming to grips with this negative behavior has changed me tremendously for the good. I thank God for His gracious patience with me.

Brokenness of Sin

It is fundamentally important to know when and where brokenness originated. It began in God's garden of perfection. It involved His perfect creation of mankind. It had to be the most beautiful experience and relationship ever known. God, the Creator, communed with them directly. Adam and Eve were a perfect reflection of the image of God. And then it happened. Through deception and disobedience, this image was forever shattered. It was broken. Their eyes were open to who they really were, and the voice of God frightened them incredibly. They hid. The relationship they once had experienced with God was broken. Their innocence was lost, and the depravity of man was inaugurated. This inherited depravity from the fall of man has forever marred the beauty of His creation. Every child to be born into this world is headed in the wrong direction. The natural bent within man is to go away from God, not toward Him. This brokenness of the soul because of sin is the root for all kinds of negative experiences humanity encounters. We cannot escape the hurt and pain from sin. This evil is engulfing the whole world. We are surrounded by wickedness and all sorts of vice. These expressions of sin are what creates the hurt and pain of brokenness. Because of this universal brokenness from sin, human reaction to these acts of wrong only create additional conflict and more brokenness. It is like a vicious cycle with a never-ending story.

The brokenness from sin is an ever-present reality. The principle of sin has made its imprint upon every fabric of our human existence. There is no component of man that does not experience this negative stamp. Scripture reminds us that *"all have sinned and fall short of the glory of God"* (Rom 3:23 ESV). Human judgment is flawed because of sin. The appetites of the flesh yield fruit that is corrupt. Selfishness is the god that has replaced the rightful place where Jehovah God needs to be. Pride is the manifested fruit of an exaggerated image of self. The Apostle Paul wrote, *"Now the works of the flesh are evident: sexual immorality, impurity, sensuality, idolatry, sorcery, enmity, strife, jealousy, fits of anger, rivalries, dissentions, divisions, envy, drunkenness, orgies, and things like these"* (Gal. 5:19–21 ESV). The Apostle declares that those individuals who do these things will not inherit the kingdom of God. This is not an exhaustive listing of wickedness, but it is pretty thorough. Sin has broken the relationship that God and man once enjoyed in the Garden of Eden. Sin is what still breaks the relationship between God and man. Sin fights against God and righteousness. Sin is a heavy taskmaster. The habits of sin are chains that hold us captive to the tyranny of Satan. No man can deliver himself from this prison of darkness.

Can you not see the problems that sin creates? The violence in our streets is a sin problem. It is the reason for the crumbling of the family and homes which are broken for irreconcilable differences. It is a sin problem. Our prisons are full because sin put them there. Choices have consequences; the reward of choosing sinful practices is a life full of brokenness. We may endeavor to dismiss the sin problem of the soul, but denial never erases the depravity of man. Sin cannot be reformed; it must be removed. Sin is a heavy burden that no one can cast aside. There has to be a Savior, our Redeemer, who alone can deliver us from this bondage.

Sin cannot be reformed; it must be removed.

Understanding this part of each person is crucial to analyzing the other aspects of brokenness. The inflicting pain against us comes from the sinful practices of another. This brokenness from others is rooted in the wretchedness of sin. When we are the inflictor of pain, it comes from the same cause, sin. Sin is our enemy, and Satan is the ruler of all darkness. The devil is the enemy of every man, woman, boy, and girl; it's not the neighbor down the street, or the person living under the same roof. Satan uses the neighbors and some of the closest to our hearts to send daggers to our core, but the reason behind the trauma of brokenness is the attack of our spiritual enemy through the channel of sinful behaviors. He fights against any individual desiring to follow God, and he does everything possible to keep a person enslaved to the habits of sin. Sin and all its effects are a big deal and are the fundamental reason for all the hurt and pain in the world. However, there still is hope. The end of the story of sin has already been written. Sin and death have been defeated. Satan was defeated, and sin was conquered. There is deliverance in our Redeemer and Savior, Jesus Christ. You can be an overcomer.

Allow me to tell you a true story. I am not proud of this account, and I have found forgiveness. O, how I struggled for years. I was a teenager and found employment in a farm setting. I worked on different farms as a young boy, but this was different. It was while endeavoring to do some farm chores with fellow workers that a scenario arose about shooting a certain bird of prey. I had developed an enjoyment of hunting, and I could shoot fairly well. As this bird of prey was perched high on a distant tree limb, the discussion was whether or not anyone could hit it. Feeling a bit boastful, I declared that I could. I was handed the gun and took my aim. The shot rang out and the bird ruffled its feathers. A surprised laughter rose from the group that it had to be close, but it was oh so far. "Try again" was the encouragement, and I took aim once more.

As I settled in for the shot, immediately my conscience said, *Don't do it.* I paused, took a deep breath, and held it. My conscience was a battleground for what was right and my pride and ego. I justified my reasoning and pulled the trigger. In the far distance, the feathered prey slipped from its perch and pummeled lifeless to the ground. The high fives and praises were quickly darkened by the heaviness that swept over my spirit. I had succumbed to the temptation, and my pride led me to a great fall. I did not want to talk about it. In fact, my continuance revealed the conviction in my spirit. I had broken man's law and God's law. Sin had broken me.

For the next several years, every time I saw a hawk of any kind, the oppression of condemnation swept in quickly. I tried to dismiss it. I tried to ignore it. I even defended my actions. I even prayed and declared to myself that it was taken care of; it was over. However, God did not let me go. Later, I find myself in a pastoral position endeavoring to tell others how they should live. My attempt at praying was clouded by visions of hawks. I wrestled with the potential consequence if I made it right. I could face a hefty fine and lose my hunting privilege as well. On every occasion of serious spiritual visitation from God, I was heavy-laden with guilt. It was time to surrender and confess. I made the call—no answer. So I began to pen a letter, in detail of the crime, the time, and all mitigating circumstances of the event. I sat and reread the letter more than once. Finally, I folded it and sealed it in the envelope. Before I walked to the mailbox, I knelt in my office and prayed, confessed, and asked God for forgiveness for my delay in restitution. I prayed for the game warden who would read the letter. I was willing to accept the consequence that would follow. As I walked the sidewalk to the mailbox, I prayed with every step I took. I placed the envelope with my sealed confession and raised the flag. As I closed the lid, a surreal peace flooded my being, and I knew the guilt was lifted. Just to prove that it pays to obey, I waited for a couple of weeks and I received a written response. I just knew a fine would be enclosed and a date set to appear in a magisterial court. Instead, it was an unimaginable letter. God was already working on the other end long before my letter arrived. God used my honest confession, my admission of guilt, acceptance of penalty, and testimony of grace from God to speak directly into the heart of the warden. God was taking this warden on his own spiritual journey. God's ways are always right.

The brokenness in my life was of my own making. My choices led to unnecessary conflict and frustration. I had no one to blame but myself. Sin never pays. It always destroys. I found triumph from this brokenness from sin in the forgiveness of Jesus Christ. Sin had met its doom.

Brokenness Has a Story

Beyond the scope of sin and the fallenness of man, what might be a principal cause for any individual experiencing this reality of brokenness? Brokenness is real. We are not conjugating a story. We know the details of our brokenness, and yet there are parts of our brokenness that remain a mystery. Our story of brokenness is etched upon our internal disk; it's engraved upon our memory bank. These memories continue to replay on the screen of our minds. It screams out for attention, but we are too scared to face it. It's raw. It's heavy. It causes us to stumble at so many different levels of interaction with fellow man. For fear of being misunderstood in so many different ways, we remain silent and carry this dark cloud everywhere we go. Whenever a crisis arises, we fall back to this same default coping mechanism. We have learned to survive. It may not be accurate or true. It more than likely is a negative learned behavior. But it is our story. It tells our story.

One of the major considerations to brokenness is the traumatic events that forever alter our lives. It shatters us inwardly. It affects us outwardly and prohibits us from processing the rest of life in a healthy manner. These types of events are what cause PTSD, post-traumatic stress disorder. In the most severe cases, PTSD disrupts cognitive behavior, making an individual unable to function in a healthy manner. We readily associate this internal brokenness to our veterans and the consequences of war. Our precious men and women have seen, heard, smelled, and done things no human should have to endure. There is nothing pleasant with war, and it deeply affects individuals. These recorded memories of war are a revolving loop of terror and horror on the mind. Every component of human DNA is directly impacted by this kind of traumatic event. For sure, it is one of the Big T of traumatic experience. You do not have to be a veteran of war to suffer from PTSD. Neither do you have to be a veteran to suffer from this catastrophic measure of brokenness. There are multiple vocations that consistently face traumatic situations—these situations are the causes for one to suffer. The field of first responders has seen a major rise in suicides because they are overcome with the stress and this debilitating condition. PTSD is cruel and most often cannot be overcome without some type of outside intervention. We have probably all known someone, or have seen someone who is suffering with these constant flashbacks of trauma. When it occurs close to home or in the immediate family, there develops a new sympathetic understanding of the sufferer. Time may bring a measure of recovery, but the memories still haunt these delicate situations.

As a mental health and peer member of a CISM Team, Critical Incident Stress Management team, I have worked firsthand with first responders who are struggling with a traumatic experience. Those stories are endless, and the details are riveting. The field of volunteers in first-responder services is in serious decline. Even those who may work for a paid service are working an exorbitant number of hours to keep emergency services available. It is only a matter of time before the level of stress reaches a breaking point, and the crumbling effect of brokenness reaches beyond a personal application. Family members and coworkers feel the effects of this kind of brokenness from traumatic experiences. The fallout can be devastating which creates more trauma and crisis experiences that contribute to the problem of being broken.

Is there anything more personally felt than the crisis of physical afflictions? When the physical health is broken, so are other aspects of the image to one's wholeness. We face questions and make decisions that may forever change our normal into something we struggle to comprehend. Our physical health is mysterious, linked to so many other aspects of our lives. Our emotions seem to be directly linked to our health, especially when sickness arises. Mood swings go with the increase or decrease in physical stamina. Physical health affects the psychological dimension of a person, and when the duration of physical ailments is extended, thoughts are entertained to one's personal worth and value. Depression is one of the direct results of physical brokenness that has impacted our psychic. Modern medicine has taken mankind to a whole new level of philosophical discussions. What is ethical and morally correct finds its moorings in one's belief system. When the spiritual side of human existence is void of God or any standard of morality, the outcomes of this kind of debate are devastating.

We dread hearing of some debilitating disease or the word cancer. It is like a terminal sentence of death. If even the mercy of God grants a reprieve or remission, there are still emotional scars from the experience. The list of side effects from the treatments for a diagnosis of cancer also bear their own stigma. It alters the appearance that we have grown accustomed to seeing. There are also sudden alterations in physical health. Accidents of all kinds have severed limbs or placed individuals in wheelchairs for life. There are sudden onsets of critical physical problems such as strokes and cardiac arrests. It changes everything instantly—no time to prepare, just lots of time to adjust. There are lessons to learn to talk, walk, and perform the basic functions of life. These kinds of traumatic experiences steal the image of wholeness and leave one with a broken image that they have to learn to accept. One of the haunting questions a person constantly wrestles with is this: *What will the new normal be?*

The table of my physical health was turned in the fall of 2021 as I came down with the coronavirus. Up to this point, I was mostly healthy. I was not on any medications, nor was I regularly needing to see a doctor. In a rather short time—days, to be more precise—I went from minor symptoms of a seasonal cold/flu to struggling to catch my breath. Things became serious in a hurry. I can only relate of a few details from what I was told. I do not remember a lot of this experience. I know now that my O_2 saturation was only 42 when I entered the local emergency room. They immediately wanted to put me on a ventilator, but somehow, I was able to refuse. I had heard of no positive outcomes from that particular step of treatment. They could not understand how I was still semi-conscious. I cannot explain it either. I was flown from that hospital to a larger facility with trauma care. There was a week plus that passed by as I lay on the brink of death. It was a scary time for my wife and family, and yet I knew nothing of those beginning days. I began to regain my cognitive ability, and I slowly realized the gravity of the situation. I could die. What will happen to my family? How will the church adjust to the death of their pastor? Every moment of my life was a gift from God. What was this process of dying going to be like?

I was going to try and fight to survive, but I was so weak and didn't know if I could fight. I had to trust that God knew where I was, and whatever He chose, I was content. It would be His plan and not my own. It is wonderful to have peace in the midst of a crisis. A miraculous turn in my battle with COVID took place as a result of a community prayer meeting. The churches in my little town and my friends got on their knees and petitioned the Heavenly Father for a miracle. They agreed in prayer, and God granted their petition. In less than twelve hours from this volume of prayer, I drastically took a turn toward recovery. God turned the switch and began to write a different ending to my near-death experience. In five days from that unity of prayer, I was at home sitting in my recliner. I came home on 6L of oxygen, but in less than four weeks, I had weaned myself from depending on this supplemental air. I lost so much from this near-death experience. I was exhausted, weak, and emotionally spent. I had no endurance to walk but a few shuffled steps. The recovery process has had its own seesaw routine, and it's still an ongoing process.

It was an overwhelming experience. My health broke, and the result from this experience has affected me in multiple dimensions. I probably will never be the same. For sure, I have a new perspective on life and what is truly important. You see things in a different dimension. Without a doubt, I am a walking, talking, breathing miracle, and I cannot tell you the reason why. It alone is in the hands of the Miracle Maker who gave me another opportunity to share the Good News of Jesus Christ. My daily trust in the Almighty has a brand-new perspective. It's a story that I will be telling of the power of prayer and the grace and mercy of my God.

The loss of life is always difficult. For people of faith, there is hope of a reunion in heaven that makes the processing of death a bit more palatable. The sting of death is real. It forever takes our loved ones from us here in this life and transports them to the eternal. The struggle in processing death is that no one returns to tell us what this one step to infinity is like. We have said our goodbyes to every possible relationship we ever knew. Grandparents, to whatever degree, are typically our first encounter with death. Age does not lessen our sorrow of loss. When the pain of loss reaches into our lives and takes our parents, siblings, or child, it greatly disrupts our functionality. When death occurs from an accident, we find it difficult to accept, and we cannot seem to find closure. We never had a chance to express love or to say any kind of farewell. It was an instantaneous snatch leaving behind a huge vacancy. We were unprepared, but we are thrust into a new reality and a new normal. The process of grief is a journey that takes time. The brokenness from loss is never erased. We feel the loss and see the loss. It is constantly before us. What we do with it determines which side of the coin of brokenness will we live.

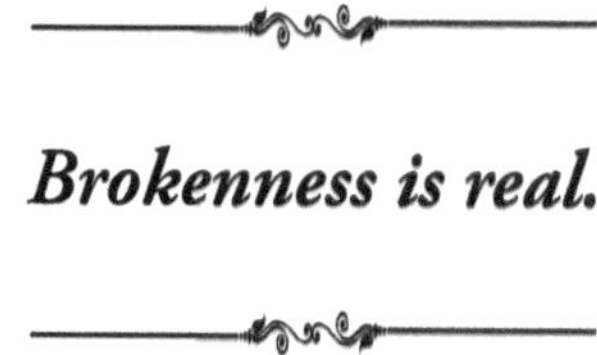

Brokenness is real.

I will never forget the day when I entered the covenant of marriage. I am forever thankful to God for allowing me to be blessed with a beautiful, God-fearing wife. Together, we entered ministry and continue to do so. It has been an eventful journey for over thirty years. I want to take you back to the beginning of those years.

We were married on the hottest summer day of the summer, I believe. The cake melted, and we couldn't keep the punch cold to save our lives. It was early in the fall of that same year when we were overjoyed to know we were having a baby. We waited a bit to share the news until we knew for sure, but the news was a delight to all. We had turned the corner from Thanksgiving and were heading into the festivity of Christmas, my favorite time of year. I was in my final year of Bible College and was also preaching in a tiny country church a few hours from home. Every weekend, we would make the journey together and share the Good News of Jesus. There were living quarters on the second floor, and the church was on the first floor.

My wife was not feeling well and could not make it for evening service. I was partway through the service when my wife, very pale in complexion, entered the back door and handed me a note and quickly retreated. I was in shock as I read the note. Serious complications had developed, and it appeared the pregnancy was in serious jeopardy. I immediately dismissed service and prepared to make the two-hour journey home. We were both in tears. It is so real to this day. As we held hands and sang "Silent Night, Holy Night," I drove like a madman toward the hospital near our home. Examination and tests revealed the pregnancy was over. The words from the doctor were like daggers of steel being thrust into our soul. He was not very comforting to our situation. He was not sympathetic to these young kids. We were in shock. How in the world would we tell the news we had lost our child in a miscarriage? However, our drama was far from over.

The following day we made our way to her parent's place, so she could be with her mother, naturally, and she wanted me to go hunting with my father-in-law for an evening hunt. I was not too focused, and we both returned to her sister's place where we were told to immediately call her mom. Something was wrong. My wife was very sick, and upon evaluating what was happening, it appeared my wife was going into labor. How? We were already told it was over. I called the ER of the hospital and they told us to quickly return. Again, we made the drive to be told again that all was over. Her sickness had subsided, and we made our way home.

It was now a Tuesday, and my parents invited us for supper because of the trauma of the past several days. As we were preparing for dinner, my wife needed to use the restroom. I became concerned because she was not coming. I knocked on the door and heard the soft reply that I needed to enter. With fear written across her countenance, she informed me that she passed something and was too afraid to look. It will be an image forever stamped on my mind. I held in the palm of my hand, an identifiable baby. I was holding our little girl for the first and last time. I wish now I had done a burial, but we were young, learning how to process life and now death. We once again returned to the hospital, and our little precious girl was handed to them. She was gone and we had suffered a loss. Christmas is still so special and the song "Silent Night" still floods our hearts and faces with tears. The trauma of death changes people.

I was now twenty-one. I had completed my undergraduate studies with a bachelor's in Ministerial Studies. I have now entered the ministry, and it was then I encountered one of those impressionable firsts. It was a death. I was asked to officiate this solemn event, but it was beyond normal. What makes this situation a traumatic event for me was that the deceased was also twenty-one. There were so many dynamics to this situation that it would take too much space to share and probably shouldn't for the integrity of the individual and family. This traumatic event, as a result of a vehicular accident, turned into a monstrosity of a funeral. Well over one thousand people paid their respects, and the funeral home was packed beyond capacity with over three hundred grieving people. As my wife I and shuffled our way to the front of the room, the heaviness of the hour hovered over my spirit. My lovely wife had to stand by my side the entirety of the service. Our backs were pushing against the casket, and I was fearful we would topple the whole thing. Our toes were very close to touching the feet of the family as they sat directly in front us, just a few inches away. Emotions were all over the place for those grieving; so were my emotions. You know how they say that when certain traumatic events happen, you can name the place and surrounding circumstances? I, too, can tell you exactly where I was when I broke. I was physically altered and emotionally spent as a result of this experience.

I was driving a school bus to supplement my income and was asked to take a field trip to a local university. This happened between the day I was notified of the death and day of the service. As I lay in my bus wrestling with my thoughts of what I could possibly say to these heartbroken lives, I was overwhelmed with nausea and sickness. I cried more tears than I ever knew possible. I suffered for days, yeah, weeks, following, and to this day, my physiological breakdown has continued to be a setback to a particular component of my health. I remember the details of this traumatic event like it was just a short time ago; it has been almost thirty years since this untimely death. The trauma of brokenness can last a lifetime.

Ministry has taken me to the bedsides of many. I have stood in hospitals and homes as those final fleeting breaths are taken. To this very moment, every death brings flashbacks to a previous occasion, and yet each new loss has created its own set of riveting memories and portraits. Life is so precious. We do our best to hold on to life forever, but death rips it from our grasp. We are left with memories of what was. How do you console a grieving mother whose premature infant lay in an incubator, waiting for the toxic salt from underdeveloped skin to poison this tiny heart to death? How do you comfort a family who has surrounded their dying loved one, now in the torments of their mind from the history of the life they lived? What words can you say to a grieving dad and family whose teenage son/brother was killed in a motor vehicle accident, fleeing the police because they stole the truck? Death brings a brokenness that many suffer for long periods of time. They get stuck in the grieving process and become handicapped in their minds of moving forward.

Culture and our living environment greatly influence our ability to process trauma productively. While there are direct teaching moments as a child, not all lessons learned are because we were purposefully taught. We have indirectly learned by observation. As a child grows through different age groups, those untaught lessons of life begin to be implemented in our decision making. The very reason a child acts out is not necessarily because of being undisciplined; he or she displays this negative behavior because of the attention they receive. True, this attention may not be a cherished response, but it still provides the attention that has been so deficit in his life. This child reasons that if I misbehave, the teacher or babysitter will give me some attention. This child will endure the punishment, but it's the attention the child wanted all along. This internal craving comes from a perceived neglect. It may not even be a true perception on the part of the child, but it does present itself as an inward brokenness to him/her personally. His default behavior is rewarded by attention.

As your story is being written, the results of traumatic events are not always immediately felt. Often, an individual will repress or stuff those emotional feelings and responses as far back into their memory as possible. Out of mind, out of sight is the denial mechanism of coping. This repressive tactic is often found used when confronted with the hidden kinds of trauma. We called them Little T's. Physical, verbal, and sexual abuse victims remain silent far too long. It is too painful to talk about it, or it is too humiliating to discuss it. They will often blame themselves for this kind of traumatic event. This continual repressive response builds layers upon layers of scars. With each layer, the brokenness becomes more intense. A momentary glimpse into these layers is when there is an outburst of words that is not typical. This burst of anger is like the burst of steam from the pressure cooker on the stove. It needs to release enough to keep it from blowing its lid. Immediately, the individual retreats back into their safe place like a turtle ducking back into its shell. They do not want to stick their neck out any more than necessary. It is all about survival.

For a person as myself, who has functioned on a performance-based thought process, the perception of failure is huge. Failure is a personal perception. There doesn't have to be any legitimacy to its reality. It is a larger umbrella that has many varied tenants that keep this negative thought process quite active. Some of these tenants are disappointments, rejection, disagreements, or conflicts. Any time one of these different elements of life present themselves, we take the full blow of failure to heart and mind. It doesn't matter if you are innocent or guilty; we have failed in our performance of duty. We blame ourselves; we are the victim to our own destructive failure perception.

As young men launching into ministry, there were lofty goals and dreams flooding our minds. We set out to be successful in our own field of labor. And then we met people. Not everyone was as convinced or excited about my ideals. In fact, they rejected them outright. I was defeated. There was a reality about life and ministry I had failed to learn in my classroom studies. I was probably too busy people pleasing in the bubble of Bible college to grasp the intensity of ministering to people. I had stepped from the halls of learning with all I needed to know to be a Minister of the Word, only to find I didn't know as much as I thought I did. This is not to blame my alma mater; it was my grandeur of lofty expectations that was struck down by the reality of people. These new people were not as awe-struck with me. My position was not on their pedestal of greatness. My performance was now scrutinized by individuals who were not integrated with a spiritual atmosphere, but by a cruel world of brokenness. Now, the brokenness in my life's story had begun, and I was not prepared to know how to process it.

I can remember the elated feeling of being voted onto a particular board. I had arrived, so I had thought. I had performed well enough to be deemed worthy of such a position. I was accepted. Remember the Proverb, *"Pride goes before destruction, and a haughty sprit before a fall"* (Pr. 16:18 ESV). I was about to crash and did not realize it, nor was I expecting to tumble. It was a short year because the next year of voting, I was voted off that board. I was crushed inwardly. My personal pride took a fatal hit. I vividly remember when some others suddenly realized I was gone that my value to them, to the board, was expressed. It may not had been what I was expecting to hear because it became evident I had been there for their use and not for my worth. I had lost the contest of popularity. In the moment, the plethora of kind words were shallow. The brokenness of being rejected was real. I am sure it was never the intention to deliberately reject; it was how it was presented. I want to believe their kind words were genuine. However, their life moved onward without me, and I was now wrestling with a failure in my mind from a negative vote. Being left alone on the side of life's highway can be overwhelming to process.

The purest of intentions will never erase the brokenness from conflict. Conflict is a disagreement on steroids. Both positions are adamantly convinced their opinion is correct. Unfortunately, when these conflicts arise, it distorts reasoning and corrupts interpretation from further situations. Conflict or disagreements are not inherently wrong. It is okay to be different or have differing opinions or positions. What becomes wrong is the accusations that develop once you are convinced your position is true. The grid of opiniated interpretation leads to some severe traumatic events. Does ministry ever have conflicts? Do fish swim in water? We do not like to think of ministries or churches facing conflict, but they do. Sometimes these conflicts are so intense and unresolvable that there are separations. New organizational structures and institutions have been born because of conflict. A situation of conflict was a breaking point in my story of brokenness. The pain was like nothing ever experienced before. It was a personal attack. Accusations are one thing, but when you know they are untrue, it is a compound burden of brokenness.

It all began with a letter; a note supposedly expressing spiritual concern, but was laced with serious attacks against the integrity of the recipient. This kind of cowardly attack is so unfortunate. It was a leap of assumptions that became evidence in the mind of the author of this accusatory note. I vividly remember the bitter wail of tears and watched my precious wife throw herself over the altar. We cried and we prayed together…then cried and prayed some more. We were blindsided by this unfortunate letter; had no hint anything of the sort was on its way. We were still recovering from some traumatic experiences from when my wife's health broke. We had not recovered to a healthy state of mind and now there was an attack against her, her relationship with God, and my pastoral leadership. This was intensely devastating.

The whole debacle continued to spiral downward and out of control. Secret meetings and discussions were happening regularly without myself, nor my wife present. The only words we were being told was something else we were doing wrong or had done wrong. Days turned to weeks, and weeks built into months. The longer this conflict arose, the more depressed I became. This was not going to end well, and the information now being passed my direction was going to be the request to resign my position or other serious determining factors were going to be engaged. I truly had not known of anything I had done wrong to bring such drastic measures. The accusations were unfounded, and the reactions to their predetermined opinions were unbiblical. This was not going to end well, and even if we could remain, my ministry was over. I had to resign. My family needed me to resign.

There were all kinds of emotional and physical stresses occurring simultaneously. We were sick. We were devastated and heartbroken. For me personally, I had utterly failed. I was convinced I missed my calling. I was a horrible pastor and person. The lies were convincing me I had nothing—I would be nothing. It was over, and I would walk away never to return to ministry again. I cannot even express in words the emotional turmoil I was battling. But God knew where I was, and He knew everything my little family was enduring. At the exact time, God sent an angel of light and a messenger of hope. A visiting evangelist who was previously scheduled came to the church for a special meeting and immediately perceived our brokenness. We sat around our dining room table until the early hours of the morning as he poured love and graciousness into our lives. He was a lifesaver, and over the next several days, God began the process to restore what was broken. As I look back in retrospect, God had allowed this measure of brokenness because He had a new level of ministry I could never have reached if I was not broken.

Secondhand Brokenness

We have heard the perils of secondhand smoke. It could seriously impair your health. You personally may not have participated in the habit of smoking, but the smoke from others could cause you complications if you were consistently ingesting their exhale. It even sounds serious. The concept of secondhand brokenness is the personal effects of another person's traumatic experience. It is along the same aspect as national disasters like floods, tornadoes, or larger scale events. You may not be directly impacted, but the exposure is being personally felt. The fallout from wars, the COVID pandemic, and the events of 9/11 would be similar to this secondhand concept. It may take several large-scale events for one to experience any direct effects from being broken. Fear, worry, and anxiety would be the leading contributor to secondhand brokenness. However, when another individual close in relationship or proximity experiences a traumatic experience, there is an element that you also encounter some similar side effects.

Following the leading of the Lord, we left the pastorate and headed full-time into an evangelistic ministry. We crisscrossed the

US from Upstate New York to the sunshine state of Florida, to the western border of Illinois and to the Atlantic coast. I believe we were in most of the states within those geographical borders. We were busy in ministry, but we were increasingly growing wearier, especially my wife. As the doors to our evangelistic ministry surprisingly began to close, God opened another door to once again assume the responsibilities of pastoring. It was the providential goodness of God because it was in this particular setting, with the availability of medical insurance, that the trauma of physical affliction hit my wife.

There is no way to tell the full details of this traumatic experience that spanned the period of almost four years. It began as we were trying to address the severe pain in her jaw. It was discovered that a disabling bone disorder had actually caused a significant distortion to her facial construction. It would take some significant preparation before surgery could be performed. In the meantime, ministry would take us to Grand Bahama to preach and sing in a camp meeting. The flights to and from there were extremely painful for my wife. She was doubled over in pain. While in the Bahamas, we discovered a significant lump behind her ear. Once we returned, we immediately visited the doctor who also immediately called a colleague. Her facial surgery was put on hold until we had answers to this lump. Tests only revealed some type of mass. Ear surgery had to be performed. Deep concern developed rapidly. The one- to two-hour procedure turned into almost five hours as I paced the OR waiting room. They must have discovered something serious. Yes, there was a lot involved, but nothing life sentencing. He only cut her ear off, glued it back on, but that was after he totally rebuilt her inner ear. Her problem was actually a direct result of the bone disorder in her face which caused other serious complications in her ear. The flight to the Bahamas had actually caused intense pressure and swelling that formed the lump. I sure hope they glued the ear to align with her other one.

We could now proceed with the facial reconstruction surgery. Five plates and twenty-seven screws later, she had it completed, but a whole new look. The recovery from that trauma entails an emergency call in the middle of the night to the doctor. Suffice it to say, when you cannot breathe for your mouth wired shut and sinuses filled with blood clots from the facial reconstruction, it is a traumatic experience when you cannot get enough air. More recovery, but this process only left her waking up with bloodstains on her pillow. More tests, but God had his hand in it all. It appeared her long-term use of pain medication was leading to ulcer activity in her stomach. An ultrasound would confirm or deny these suppositions.

Into the lab once again for this benign imaging. All those hopes were thrown to the wind as the technician discovered "by accident" an excessive amount of fluid around the heart. She was on the verge of congestive heart failure if it was not addressed immediately. The technician ordered us STAT to the hospital for further imagining of the heart. We have now gone from the stomach to the heart. This was a bit more serious. Tests, on two separate occasions, revealed two significant holes in her heart. The blood was shunting back and forth in the upper chambers. CHF was imminent, and if not corrected before that happens, there was no opportunity available for repair.

To the amazement of the doctors, they could not understand how she had given birth naturally to two children. She was told she should have died in the delivery room. I guess God had other plans. Our plans were now facing an open-heart procedure. The doctors informed us that when you invade the interior of the heart, it is still an open-heart procedure even though the chest may not have been split open. We had to sign and give the okay for a split sternum in case this new way of procedure malfunctioned.

Guess what? There was a malfunction. It was a different type of malfunction. The anesthesiologist was too busy reading his magazine and did not fully sedate my wife, and she woke up in the middle of the procedure. It was traumatizing to her to see her heart on the monitor directly above her head, hear the doctors talking code and feeling the sensation of the instruments moving inside her as they were deploying the Amphlatzer Occluder device to close her atrial septum defect. Complications arose during the suturing of the femoral artery, and a blood clot formed. She was now going into a measure of shock as her body began to convulse on the table. Medicines and fem-stop were used to stop the bleeding. I was summoned to go back and see her, and she burst into tears as my face appeared around the curtain. She was waiting any moment to slip away.

I tried to console her, but the traumatic experience was a bit overwhelming. She requested to be able to go to the restroom, but I told her she was not allowed to move. She was insistent and after several elevated attempts to secure help, a nurse finally showed up to bring the needed assistance. As she pulled back the sheet, she swore and immediately went into a state of emergency interventions. What we did not know then, was the fem-stop had malfunctioned, and my wife was profusely bleeding to death. It was a matter of moments before she would go to sleep, never to awake. Her insistence to being relieved saved her life. The reason for the development of her necessity was the nurse had failed to slow the medicine flow in the IV. It was left wide open and my wife truly was not bluffing when she stated…*I have to go now*! You see, God was intervening every step of the way. Her recovery process led into another cardiac situation, and we were ordered via phone to immediately head to the emergency room. The doctor called back and said to forget that step and go directly to the cardiac floor. I have a bed waiting for you. Again, my wife headed back into the OR and another procedure had to be done. Four major surgeries and lots of drama and traumatic experiences later, she has learned to live with her current situations. Every step of the way, I was by her side. I did not go under the surgeon's knife or face the same paths my wife had to endure, but I was secondhand traumatized as I walked this valley with her. It left its mark deeply implanted on my mind and heart. I will always remember these traumatizing experiences.

As a family, we jostled this road of bumps and potholes. Life was constantly changing. The normalcy of living was thrown out long ago. Our boys at the time were traumatized as their sweet mother lay in limbo and was constantly being "sick." They were quickly ushered into household chores at a very young age. It really didn't hurt them to do home chores, but it was the underlying reasons why it was being done that fits into our description of secondhand brokenness.

One person's emotional trauma is another person's victimization.

By calling it secondhand brokenness does not mean it is not important. It may be secondhanded in its receiving, but it is your firsthand experience. Marriage relationships become strained because sexual abuse of one of the partners creates nightmares and revisits their trauma in their marital relationships. One person's emotional trauma is another person's victimization. The trauma is not any less severe than if it was you personally encountering the crisis. In fact, the turmoil begins in how we are going to process these encounters with someone else's traumatic experience. This is how it directly starts to impact you personally. It becomes your own crisis. It totally interrupts what was routine and normal by creating your own story of being broken. One's personality can magnify the internal struggle and complicate the processing of another's pain. You can feel the hurt so deeply that it impedes normal activities such as diet and sleep. You take this hurt and pain upon yourself even though it did not directly happen to you. We call these individuals an empath. Such a characteristic can be comforting to others, but it traumatizes the person who processes life's situations in this particular way of empathy. Personal emotions become attached to the crisis of another and now becomes personally real to themselves.

PART TWO

The Triumph Over Brokenness

A Journey Begins

The team is down to the last batter. It's the bottom of the ninth and the score is tied, but the winning run is standing on third. You step toward the plate and place your feet inside that batter's box. The game is resting on your shoulders. But this game isn't just a game. It is the final game of the World Series. The stats tell us the series is tied at three games apiece. Why does it have to be me coming to the plate? You haven't had the best record under stressful circumstances. You know you will strike out and send it into extra innings. Failure looms heavy; it has happened before. The pitcher looks directly into your eyes. He is reading you like a book, or so it seems. He gestures that he has his eye on you. It's intimidating. Your stance, the pitch—"*Strike!*" The sound of the umpire's voice sends chills down your spine. Again, another pitch. "*Ball,*" he bellows. Thanks, I am buying a little more time, at least until the inevitable. If another strike is called, fear will grip so tight. I will not be able to breathe let alone bat. You step out of the batter's box and turn toward the coach. The coach calls a time-out and walks toward you. In hushed tones, he speaks words of encouragement.

He says, "I have confidence in you. You can do this. Don't worry about the outcome. Just do what you know you can do. Swing that bat and let the ball go on its own. You got this." He pats your shoulder and turns and walks back towards the dugout. You step toward the batter's box again, just hoping to make a connection. It seems like it takes forever for the pitcher to wind up and send the ball toward home plate. You hardly see it coming, but the bellow from the umpire pierces once again. "*Strike!*"

What! How can this be? Now you're behind on the count, and it is only a matter of time. "*Ball 2,*" the umpire declares. "*Ball 3,* Full Count!" This is it. The last pitch. It's all or nothing. By this time the whole stadium is on their feet. The emotions are mixed, but you know how desperately you feel on the inside. You just want a hit into the outfield. That will score the winning run. You ready yourself and wait for the pitch. If it is anywhere close to the strike zone, you are swinging away. *Crack*…the ball ricochets foul. Again, you step toward the plate and ready your gaze on the pitcher and the incoming fast-ball. You see the windup and the hurling round object heading your way. *Crack* once again, and the ball heads directly toward third base. You beat it toward first with the hope you can outrun the gun of the third baseman. It's going to be close for sure. But the throw is not on its mark, and the first baseman misjudges it completely. As the ball hurls toward the bleachers, you cross the plate, totally elated in the error, but delighted to know you didn't cause the last out and the runner on third easily scored the winning run. Go ahead, celebrate the win! It was a victory for you, the team, even though you had not always performed well at the plate.

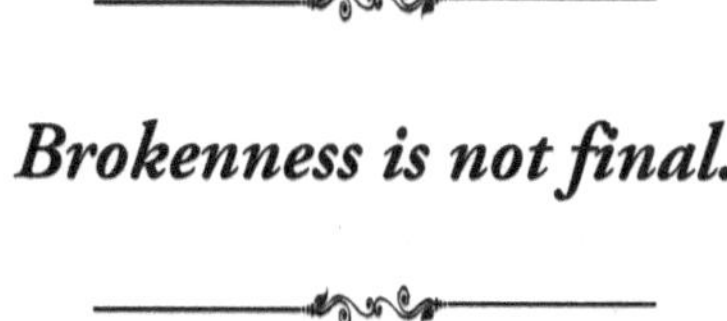

Brokenness is not final.

Life is filled with ups and downs; crisis after crisis; trauma after trauma, mingled with a few scenes of breathtaking beauty. When the events of a traumatic experience occur, it is like the stress of the batter in the last inning, with the last out, with the last pitch. You cannot escape from the responsibility of the moment. You have to do something, but what can you do?

Brokenness is not final. Your story does not have to end in the pit of despair. The accusations of failure do not define you as a person; it may just describe a specific situation. No one ever gets it right all the time. There is no element of infallible perfection known to mankind. There is only One who is perfect, and His name is Jesus Christ. What is so important is to learn from the past, identify the source of your pain, and take those steps necessary to be the overcomer. Triumph is not an eraser; it's a minimizer. It is moving forward as you recreate a new normal with a new purpose and meaning.

Identify Your Brokenness

No one can dictate to you what your brokenness looks like in your life. Just know this: every person has a story. Their story is not yours, and your story does not belong to them. What does your story look like? If you were to write out the story of your life, what would the chapter titles be? Have you encountered some major traumatic experiences that redefined your life? Maybe there is an accumulation of all kinds of crises that have eaten away at your core. You are tired emotionally. You are exhausted physically. The hope for a new tomorrow is taken away by the pain of your past. It is an endless cycle of brokenness. Somehow, it defines you; it is your identity. I recognize the pain of telling your story or events of your brokenness, but I also know how helpful it is to admit it. The road to healing begins first with admitting there are some unresolved traumatic events. Even during the process of working through one crisis event, a past traumatic experience surfaces and becomes evident—it, too, needs to be addressed. The aspect of identifying your dynamics of brokenness is not to prescribe guilt or to point blame. It is unnecessary to point fingers. You need to focus upon you first and come to a healthy perception of who you really are. The identifying process is the attempt to realize that brokenness is present and to take the necessary steps toward the process to healing. You are not alone in this unfortunate reality, yet it is not hopeless. It is your turn to face what constantly disrupts your daily life by dragging you backward instead of moving you forward.

For the longest time, I struggled with trying to understand what was happening on the inside of me. My heart and mind were not on the same page, nor did it seem they were in the same book. What added to this turmoil was the stigma from the position I held in society. How could a person of the cloth, a man of God, be wrestling with issues of life? I was inwardly broken while functioning in ministry. I could point people in the right direction, and yet it seemed I had difficulty in following my own advice. The patience and compassion of my Heavenly Father led me all the way. He placed some individuals and circumstances in my pathway that turned my focus away from what was unhealthy toward that which is wholesome. It would be an easy solution if I could tell you there was a specific incident that happened that made all the difference. Truth be told, it actually was a learning process that eventually led me to a fresh revelation of the Person of Jesus Christ.

First, I had to face my brokenness. I had to admit to the negative thought processes. I truthfully had to retrain my mind to think differently. This was the pivotal turning point that started me in a healthy direction. It was a new and greater understanding of who Jesus is and not what I had learned He wasn't. Negative learned behavior contributes immensely to experiential brokenness. In Christ, I found my identity, and not my brokenness. Hope was reborn and the healing process continues. *"The steadfast love of the Lord never ceases; his mercies never come to an end; they are new every morning; great is your faithfulness"* (Lam. 3:22–23 ESV).

Do not be overwhelmed in the process of finding the triumph over your internal brokenness. Just know that there is healing. It is not beyond being a reality in your heart and life. We are so accustomed to having instant resolutions. The click of the computer mouse brings instant information. The push of the buttons on the microwave produces a scorching hot dish in a very short element of time. Healing takes time. Recovery is not going to happen overnight. It may take several revisits of a particular traumatic experience to upload all the stuffed and hidden details. Once it is uploaded to the front of our minds, it is then we can begin to evaluate the pain and hurt through a healthy thought process. You have to begin the process somewhere. Start by identifying the hurts and causes of your pain. Brokenness may seem like an insurmountable mountain. It looms high into the sky and disappears into the hovering clouds. It appears so massive that we are discouraged before we even try to take that first step. Go ahead; take the step. There is healing to be found.

***In Christ, I found my identity,
and not my brokenness.***

Small Steps

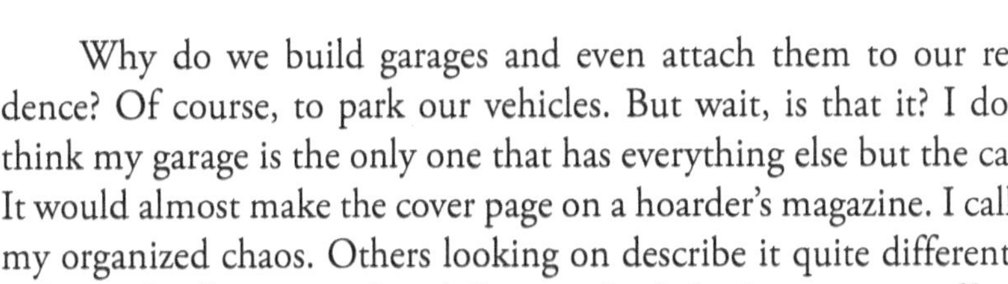

Why do we build garages and even attach them to our residence? Of course, to park our vehicles. But wait, is that it? I don't think my garage is the only one that has everything else but the cars. It would almost make the cover page on a hoarder's magazine. I call it my organized chaos. Others looking on describe it quite differently. When I finally get tired and frustrated of climbing over stuff and tripping over wood, boxes, and tools, I attempt to clean it. I stand on an elevated landing and gaze across the jungle of lost items. Where do I begin? The task is daunting and overwhelming. I have to choose to just begin. You have to start somewhere. I descend a few steps and bend over and pick up a piece of trash and wonder why I just didn't throw it in a can. Maybe it wasn't my discarded trash, but who can I blame? At this point, it's my mess; get busy and clean it up.

The same is true in our approach to overcoming the brokenness that has cluttered our hearts, our minds, and our lives. It is not a one size fits all standard of care. I assure you that the process is not the same as someone else's journey. You cannot focus or try to duplicate what another person has done. You have to make this journey your own, but you have to start. You have to begin the process to healing by taking the essential steps to talk to someone, to pray, or to find a counselor. I cannot tell you the exact order you have to take, but I do know there is one place where everyone needs to begin. You have to make this personal. It has to be real for you. Just like in building a structure of any size, you need a good foundation. Once your foundation is secure, it is then you begin to erect your brand-new edifice. The right foundation is in the person of Jesus Christ. Once this foundation is secure, He will directly align your steps to be supportive of the person of Christ and tailor-made for your specific needs. Jesus is your greatest support person and cheerleader for wholeness of life.

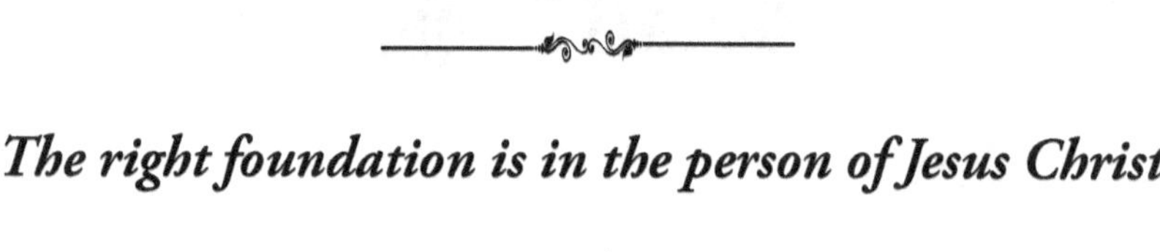

The right foundation is in the person of Jesus Christ.

Antidote for Sin

No one can master sin on their own. Sin masters you. It holds you captive and enslaves you to its habits. Since we are creatures of habit, the natural habit for all humanity is involvement in sin. We have already explored how and where sin began, but it is important to know that sin has been defeated. The chains of sin that have held mankind captive were broken and cast asunder. The doors to the prison house of darkness were opened and the light of hope shown inside. This light has led multitudes to a state of victory and triumph. The light is the Gospel of Jesus Christ. This Good News is salvation from sin. He has procured our salvation and deliverance from sin by his sacrificial atoning death on the cross. Sin and Satan were defeated triumphantly, and the resurrection is proof. This triumph of Jesus Christ is ours to experience. Have you found Him to be your personal Savior?

The struggle from sin is real, and the effects are devastating. Sin has destroyed so much and has broken the lives of many. It is sin that has turned love into lust. It is sin that has broken the covenants of marriage. Sin has broken the boundaries of morality leading to many aspects of psychological dysfunction. It is the practice of sinful behavior, with all kinds and forms of evil, that has destroyed the bodies and minds of God's created eternal beings. It is sin that steals, kills, and destroys. Humanity is the possessor of this wickedness and the propensity for evil is limitless. We must have a deliverer. Jesus is our only Redeemer. He alone is the antidote for sin. There is forgiveness in Jesus. *"If we confess our sins, he is faithful and just to forgive us our sins, and to cleanse us from all unrighteousness"* (1 John 1:9 ESV). This forgiveness lifts guilt and condemnation from our shoulders. Our past is forgiven; *"as far as the east is from west, so far does he remove our transgressions from us"* (Ps. 103:12 ESV). How well does Jesus forgive? The prophet Isaiah wrote, *"I, I am He, who blots out your transgressions for my own sake, and I will not remember your sins"* (Is. 43:25 ESV). God does not dig up our past and throw it in our face. His choice is to remove our transgressions and not remember them against us again. The enemy of our souls, Satan, is the accuser. He is forever throwing our past before us. He is constantly inflicting our minds with memories of what was. God does not do this. He forgives, period. In place of the guilt of our past, there now resides peace. The Holy Spirit of God gives us a new identity of where we belong.

Finding forgiveness is an alignment of our soul to be reconciled with God. Sin separated us from God. We were an estranged enemy of God because of sin and our disobedience toward Him. The justice of God demands a penalty for sin, but forgiveness removes it. The penalty of sin is removed from our sentencing, and our name is now recorded in the Lambs Book of Life. This is transformative to every dynamic of our lives. 2 Corinthians 5:17 says, *"Therefore, if anyone is in Christ, he is a new creation; old things have passed away; behold all things have become new"* (NKJV). Forgiveness does not erase the scars of our past, but it does birth a brand-new conduct of living. In some aspects, our minds carry the remembrance of the life we use to live. The conduct of the life controlled by sin is not a positive image, but the grace of God transforms us into a new life abiding in Christ. The joy of knowing Christ in a personal real relationship is the witness of His Spirit and the abiding peace of God. The light of hope is shining where the dread of darkness shadowed our life. This forgiveness from God does not nullify the need for civil justice or penalty for the violation of societal laws. There are consequences for sin for the choices we made, but know that whatever the consequences of our actions may require, it does not erase the presence of His grace. Grace is always greater than sin. *"But where sin abounded, grace abounded much more"* (Rom. 5:20 NKJV).

We cannot ignore this issue of sin. It is the number one problem with every individual. It is the cause of the hurt and pain and the reason such negative and evil actions transpire. Sin is a heavy burden. It breaks down every component of man. It disrupts every aspect of society. It is a major serious problem. There is nothing innocent about sin. The cause of verbal and physical abuse comes from the depraved heart of man. The devastation of sexual perversions of all kinds is rooted in this depravity of man. God did not create evil. Evil came as a result of man's choice to disobey God's command and usurp His authority for their own pleasure. Just as darkness is the absence of light, so is evil the absence of God. The only way to change the course of evil behavior is to find the redemptive work of grace in the atoning blood of our Savior Jesus Christ.

The God-shaped hole in our hearts can only be filled by God.

There is nothing tangible that can fill the void that sin created. You will frustrate yourself trying to fill this void without coming to Christ. The God-shaped hole in our hearts can only be filled by God. Trying to fill it will all kinds of other pleasures of sin only creates more heartaches, pain, scars, and brokenness. If you turn to God in faith, admit your need of a Savior, confess the awfulness of your sin, and ask for His forgiveness, it is through His mercy and grace that salvation is granted. His salvation is the gift from God and the perfect fit for that emptiness and void you had within.

Antibiotics are the medicines used to confront bacterial viruses and infections. Most often, if taken as prescribed, it will rid you of the infection that was plaguing your physical body. There might be side effects from both the infection and the medicine. Some will dissolve in time, but there can also be long-term effects. Why should you take the medicine? We desire to be rid of the sickness, pain, and fever. We trust the medical professional that he/she knows what is best. Can we not trust the plan that God has foreordained to be the remedy of the malady of sin? Jesus is not a fix for a mistake in God's creation. Jesus is the answer to man's wrong decision. The error was believing the serpent that we would become as gods knowing what is good and evil. Truth is this: we became pawns to Lucifer's self-destructive lie and enslaved us to follow the same path he had taken. It was the cause of his expulsion from heaven and now he deceived man by the same lie. You can never elevate yourself to share the place that only God Almighty can fill. But you can know the saving power of Jesus Christ who can transform your life into a beautiful testimony of His saving grace. Jesus alone is the complete antidote for sin. *"And there is salvation in no one else, for there is no other name under heaven given among men by which we must be saved"* (Acts 4:12 ESV).

The Process to Wholeness

If you could define the word perfection, how would you do it? How could you describe it? What kind of picture or image is created in your mind as you contemplate this word, perfection? If you were to Google the word perfection, you would find this definition: "the condition, state, or quality of being free or as free as possible from all flaws or defects" (Oxford Languages). Sounds legit, but I ask, who is qualifying the standard? In whose opinion is it settled that anything, or something, is perfect? Such an ideal condition rests in the perception of the individual. It might be relative to their own standard or ideal circumstances. However, if compare to another individual's perception of perfection, it may come up short, or not even come close to qualifying as perfection.

Think with me about all the entries we could list where we strive for perfection. Yeah, we demand it, and if it happens to be less than perfect, we will not provide a positive review. Our dining-out experiences need to find our food selections to be delivered to perfection. We will not accept wilted lettuce, cold steaks, or moldy desserts. The cleanliness of our medical facilities needs to be held to this standard of perfection. You would not want to be wheeled into the operation room with soiled linens lying on the floor, or bloody instruments scattered on the cart next to your operating table. Rightfully so, we demand a perfectly sterile clean environment. It is this same kind of image of perfection we envision as we approach various kinds of relationships. The selection of the perfect companion, we get the perfect job, and we go on the perfect vacation, but guess what? The person we thought would be so perfect isn't. The job we thought was the ideal perfect job is not at all what was advertised. And the vacation— well, the sunsets were not as pretty, nor was the water quite that blue. What now enters the mind are the disappointments, the complaints, and other negative responses because of our less-than-perfect dreams and choices. This danger of setting a standard of perfection by earthly measurements is it is always bound to fail. There has to be a better standard. So how can we start this process of confronting the negativity that is all around us?

The Stepping Stones
of Your Story

On more than one occasion I have been drawn to a passage of scripture that is filled with all kinds of emotions. The conflict of battles was raging, and Israel was in the attack mode. However, when they returned home, their city was burned, and their wives and children were taken captive. Can you imagine what piercing daggers were inflicting their hearts and minds? The outbursts of their anger turned, and now David their King was in the crosshairs. The sentence was that he needed to be stoned. Someone had to be blamed, so why not their leader? David had led his men away and now their very heart and soul have been ripped from their chests. In this volatile moment of brokenness from this traumatic experience, you read these words, *"…but David encouraged [strengthened] himself in the Lord his God"* (1 Sam. 30:6 NKJV/ESV). David had turned to the one place he knew where help could be found; that direction was God.

Brokenness has a way of becoming our identity. We adopt the failures of our past as being the destiny of our tomorrows. We dwell upon the disappointments and rejections as if they are the prescriptions for life. We settle for being alone because of our inability to find our voice or a listening ear. It is time to reach out and ask for help. You need to talk to somebody. Talking is a natural way of therapy. It allows the release of built-up emotions. It becomes the calming medicine for the stress-filled life. The reason talking is helpful is because of the ears that are listening. If no one is listening, talking is useless. It is when we find that person who is willing to listen to our story that the healing process can begin.

1. Look upward

First of all, talk to Jesus. He is always available. People are limited in their availability; that is why there are answering machines. God is always available. Jeremiah 33:3 says, *"Call to me and I will answer you"* (ESV). His ears are tuned for the cry of help. His eyes already see you and there is nothing hidden from Him. He is already waiting on you to call to him in prayer. Prayer is not a magic formula to be presented, but it is the language you and I use to talk to God. Talk to Him. Tell Him your story. Pour out your hurt, your pain, your rejection, your abuse. Tell him of your trauma because He knows and feels your pain. Scriptures tell us that Jesus Christ is our High Priest who sympathizes with our weaknesses. He truly understands our brokenness. Even though He knew no sin because He is the spotless, sinless, Son of God, His human embodiment allowed Him to experience all the emotional feelings that you and I also experience. He knew what temptation was. He faced satanic harassment. The Prophet Isaiah says, *"He is despised and rejected by men, a Man of sorrows and acquainted with grief. He was wounded…He was bruised… He was oppressed…He was afflicted"* (Isaiah 53). He was burdened so extremely by the weight of our sin that His physical body broke and sweat drops of blood. You know how heavy the burden of sin is in your own life—now, consider the weight of that burden and multiply it for the whole world. Is it any wonder he broke physically? *"He was bruised for our iniquities.*" He was chastised, so we could know peace. He was beaten, scourged, humiliated, and scared for our sin. He did nothing to deserve such punishment. It was all for you and I, so we can know forgiveness and the power of healing.

Talking to Jesus is what creates a new and healthy identity. When brokenness has shattered who they were, the haunting quest for so many is to discover who they have become. In many circumstances, the broken do not like who they currently are and just want to return to being comfortable. They just want to be normal and live a normal routine of life. Unfortunately, their instability erases being comfortable, and the result of this troubled path is that their value and worth evaporate. It is this communication with Jesus Christ and learning to know Him, that begins to lift and break the vicious cycles of negative coping mechanisms. The Bible says, "*Humble yourselves under the mighty hand of God, that He may exalt you in due time, casting all your care upon Him, for He cares for you*" (1 Peter 5:6–7 NKJV). Jesus has made Himself available for you as your new identity. In Christ, your value and worth are established. Your brokenness does not define you. You do not need to be bound in the shackles and burdens of your past. Your shattered dreams, plans, and wishes are replaced with a loving, caring Redeemer. He offers a new way of life filled with meaning and eternal purpose. He gives you hope because He is Hope. *"He is the Way, the Truth, the Life"* (John 14:6). He is the Passport to Heaven.

Brokenness has a way of becoming our identity.

I had tried tirelessly to create my own image yet did not realize I was on a fruitless, ambitious pursuit. It was when the crisis experiences hit that the realization became brutally evident. My performance had failed. My abilities were exhausted, and I was left broken. In my own perception, I was surrounded by the shreds of my failures. God had to allow me to hit this rock bottom before I could be built back up. I had to be honest with my own self-degrading and negative thought patterns. I needed to be helpless. I needed to sense a healthy insufficiency of my own inabilities to sustain on my own. It was in this lonely, dark meadow of brokenness that I truly saw Jesus. He wasn't condescending. He was inspiring. He was not stern, but full of compassion. He was not threatening, but inviting. This tender Jesus never reprimanded me once, but spoke graciousness like never before. I was immensely overcome by the power of His penetrating love. I never knew this kind of love. I had believed that all the love I had ever experienced I had to earn through my human abilities. All my acceptance was conditional; I had to perform well. But Jesus, He loved me; not because I was whole, but because I was broken. He branded me deeply with His love. I knew that His identity had to be my identity. For the first time, I knew that Jesus loved me, and it was not based upon any external standard of measurement. It was liberating. A huge emotional burden and a mountain of baggage rolled from my shoulders. It was a triumphant victory at last. It was a whole new beginning. Before me was the loving, gentle Shepherd. I just needed to follow His lead.

2. Ask for help

The second step and all subsequent steps need to be in accordance to the leading of the Shepherd, Jesus Christ. It is extremely helpful and important to find a person who has a listening ear and a silent tongue. Confidentiality is the first step to establishing a trusting relationship between peers. I wish I could assure you that it would not be too difficult, but invariably, finding a true confidant may take some time. Don't get too exasperated in this search. There are genuine people with open minds, listening ears, and caring hearts. Talk to your Pastor or spiritual advisor. Inquire if there has been any training in crisis intervention or therapeutic services. Not all Pastors have personal training, but they are an excellent resource to begin in talking with someone. They more than likely have a referral contact list for various services and can lead you in a healthy direction. Your Pastor does care for you. Allow him to be the caring shepherd that leads you to Jesus and encourages you to talk to other professionals to address your struggles. May that trust be never broken.

The biggest hurdle ever to overcome is the first request for help. There is a unique stigma about asking for help. So many think it is a sign of weakness. It is more a testimony of strength than it is of being a weak person. There is no individual that is beyond the need for outside assistance. You just may find it more helpful to talk to someone who is not acquainted with you than to a person who has some form of connection. When speaking with an acquaintance, there is a tendency to adjust your story to deflect away from you personally, rather than to admit to a debilitating traumatic experience. It is not easy to bear your inner soul, but if you are ever going to find triumph over brokenness, it takes complete honesty. Here is where the issue of confidentiality rests. If there is any slightest breach of this trust, the effectiveness of communication is done. Honesty will never be complete, and the truth may never be revealed.

I remember an instance when I was encouraged to share a particular situation with an individual who may have had a similar experience. I trusted because of the recommendation. I told my story, and it appeared the person listened. What did not happen was for their tongue to be silent. In fact, my story was told to the very person who had a close connection to my quandary. My trust was broken because of broken confidentiality. The hurt and pain from this incident was added to my personal struggle. For the longest time afterward, I did not share anything. I carried all kinds of experiential brokenness and stuffed it deep. It added much more internal brokenness because I could not talk to anyone to help me process my traumatic experiences.

In the process of overcoming your trauma, you may need to find a psychologist or a psychiatrist. It may be important to talk to your primary care physician. Not all emotional difficulties are a direct result to a traumatic experience. Some emotional challenges are because of a physical need. Medications can correct imbalances and level hormones which bring a surprising stability where once was a roller coaster ride. In a counseling setting, therapeutic intervention, listening, and knowledge all combined can be a healthy prescription to overcome and begin the process of healing. It may be necessary to be prescribed some medications which can also contribute a measure of help as you work through the scars and traumas of the past. Seek to overcome. Strive to get above. Don't settle for an indefinite scope of therapy. Set a goal. Reach for the goal and never stop fighting to attain your sense of wholeness. Again, never leave God behind. He truly needs to lead. Finding outside help is not a lack of faith. It is a step of faith when God is leading you. Without His leading, you are trying to solve your problem with someone or something that is limited in knowledge and ability. God is limitless. *"The things which are impossible with men are possible with God"* (Luke 18:27 NKJV).

3. Collect the tools

There are resources of written material that can complement or charter your journey of triumph. Make sure you consider my resource list at the end of this book. But I really want to share the best resource available to you. The author of this book is still alive. He has infinite knowledge in all things. There is nothing too difficult that He cannot handle. He is the Creator of all things and holds all power in His hands. He is everywhere at all times. There is no deficiency in Him. He is Eternal, and so is His Word. This resource is the Holy Bible. It is the number one best seller. Make sure you read it. Discover the tools necessary in coping with all your life's difficulties. The wisdom within those pages is life altering. It is the how-to for all aspects of our lives. It is the roadmap for heaven. Because it is inspired by the Holy Spirit, it is the best inspirational read you could ever put before your eyes. The volumes of printed resources are not equivalent in value to the Bible. Fallible men may write excellent material, but it is an infallible God who wrote this living Book. The content of God's material never changes or becomes obsolete. It is still current and vibrant. It is an eternal truth that is forever relevant. The Psalmist wrote, *"Your Word is a Lamp to my feet, and a Light to my path"* (Ps. 119:105 NKJV).

Meditate on His Word. Let his Word soak inward, all the way to your core. The Word of God is life changing. His promises are not empty words; they are anchors. Start committing verses of scripture to memory. These hidden scriptures are flash cards to be recited in the moments when your brokenness is screaming too loud. His words offer peace and direction. They are the voice of God speaking hope into our chaotic world of turmoil.

I strongly recommend listening to music that is soothing and relaxing. Don't be driven by a rhythm, but be led by a melody with supporting harmonies. Music is a therapy with universal application. The lyrics are very important, and some of the most powerful melodies of song were composed in the darkest and most traumatic experience one could imagine. Music is a language without boundaries. We may not be able to understand more than one dialect of language, but music crosses all ethnicities and is played the same all around the world. There is only one written language of music, and we can all understand it. We might be able to perform it by instrument or voice, but our ears are tuned to its frequencies, and it goes directly to our heart. In our own quietness and solitude, music can lift us directly into the presence of God, our Hope and Healer. Music can be our prayer when we cannot find the words to speak. The Book of Psalms is like a hymnbook. The composition of those verses was often used in worship. Many passages of this Psalm book speak mightily to individuals in times of discomfort. For sure, they uplift the soul.

4. Set attainable Goals

What is your goal in this recovery process? Is there a purpose in your journey to wholeness? Without setting a healthy goal and an attainable result, you are aimlessly reaching into the air hoping to catch something, but you do not know what. In your mind, what does a triumph over brokenness look like to you? Is it the correct picture? Is it healthy? I like these words from the Apostle Paul, *"Brothers, I do not consider that I have made it my own, but one thing I do, forgetting what lies behind and straining forward to what lies ahead, I press on toward the goal for the prize of the upward call of God in Christ Jesus"* (Php. 3:13–14 ESV).

There are things in our past that cannot be undone. There are experiences you cannot do over or consequences reversed. The experiences that break us need to be moved from the forefront of our focus and be replaced with the instructional truths set in God's Word. We are told to be *"Imitators of God as dear children"* (Eph. 5:1 ESV). The person of Jesus Christ must be your role model. He is the correct pattern for your life. This is the true definition of what it means to be a Christian. The writer of the letter to the Hebrews encourages us to be *"Looking unto Jesus, the Author and Finisher of our faith"* (Heb. 12:2 NKJV). This is a healthy goal to set before you as you seek to triumph over your past.

Victory is not one huge image. It is a collage of many portraits that create a greater image of wholeness. Do not despise the small victories. They still are victories. It will be the accumulation of small steps that takes us farther down the road to recovery. To set a huge goal out in front of yourself and not be able to see the progress toward that goal, will be disappointing and discouraging. However, if you set a goal closer and visualize the progress, it will encourage you to keep striving. Set another attainable goal and keep reaching. It will not be too long before a larger measure of triumph will be attained, and you can set another memorial for victory. Write down every goal and chart the progress or the journey toward that goal. Sometimes the journey has some setbacks, but there are rebounds too. Log it all down, and you will see the progress happening on paper and enjoy it experientially.

Do not despise small victories.

Celebrate every goal. It doesn't have to be outlandish celebration, but it needs to be a joyous occasion. The milestone reached is another victory and another memorial. Set out a memorial because they will be reminders to you of how far you have journeyed and what it was you have overcome. It is all part of your story. The more memorials you establish the greater your story. Every triumph is a testimony to others and yourself. Be thankful and full of praise to God. The road of brokenness is a lonely road. You are left to journey it in your own misery. However, your overcoming triumphs should be more than an individual celebration. Ask others to join with you, and in doing so, it strengthens you and encourages others.

It is better to set a goal and not be able to reach it than to not set goal and attain it. Nothing is still nothing. Your goal is something and it just might be your turning point.

5. Jump the Hurdles

As a young boy, my oldest son had an amazing ability to jump. I believe we were on a vacation, but we were at a park which had a tennis court. As we were walking around, this young fellow went running onto the court. I turned to my wife and said, "He is going to jump that net." He went running and stopped at the net. The three-foot net was chest high on this fellow. We stood and watched as he walked backward while his gaze was fixed on this hurdle in front of him. I was imagining his attempt and not quite clearing the top and face planting on the court below. He reached his calculated distance and set off on a sprint toward the net. At the precise moment, without hesitation, he leaped into the air and cleared the top of the net with sufficient distance. I was stunned as his ability to leap this hurdle that was nearly as big as he was.

I cannot tell you what hurdles you might encounter in this journey to overcome and to recover from your brokenness. I just know there will be some obstacles to overcome, some hurdles to jump, and maybe a few dark places to walk. But remember, these situations are not stopping points. They are direct points to confront and cross over. You will have to make this definite choice to persevere.

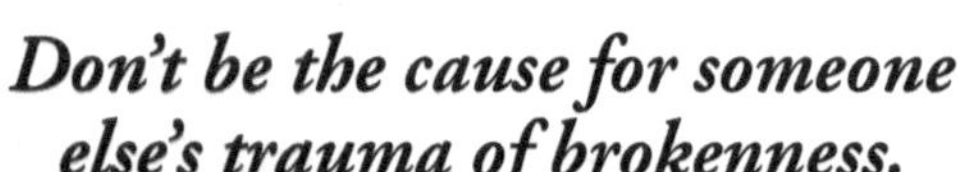

Don't be the cause for someone else's trauma of brokenness.

This recovery process is like peeling off the layers of an onion. At the very core is the traumatic experience that broke some part of you. As time passed, layer upon layer of some aspect of a coping mechanism was applied, but you never processed the cause for all those layers. As you begin your recovery, you work through those layers one at a time, and as you do, you face various aspects of emotions and conflicting messages. You cannot ignore those details; you have to confront them and work through them. You made the important choice to begin this healing process, and you must continue to choose to finish it too. You may face a hurdle of confession. It may be painful, but is necessary. There is nothing easy about admitting to anything especially if you are in the wrong. Brokenness happens from our own personal choices too. It's not always what might have happened against you. I know you will come face to face with the matter of forgiveness. The hurdle of forgiveness versus unforgiveness cannot stand in your way. You cannot sidestep this hurdle, but you must process it. Jump this hurdle by choosing to forgive. Forgiveness releases you—not an exoneration of the guilty. Forgiveness is healing. Unforgiveness keeps the wounds broken open. Bitterness is a deep infection of unprocessed hurt and pain. Nothing is more devastating than this inner sore that spews forth ugly words from our lips. The bad breath from this infection of the soul taints our attitudes and is repulsive to those around us. It separates the dearest of friends and relationships. You better jump this hurdle and overcome this virus with the antibiotic of God's grace. The hurdle of hatred and revenge must be processed as well through the grace of God. Let God take care of vengeance.

The emotional responses in this recovery process can be a woven web or a braided cord. It can be frustrating to analyze, but with every choice to choose Christ over our self, is a step in the right direction. A healthy response to every raised hackle is to face it and process it through the help of the Lord. Jump those hurdles with grace; the more you overcome, the easier the jumps become. With every hurdle crossed, the more inspiring it becomes. It's encouraging to look back across the progress thus making the choice to remain committed on this journey. Sometimes, you need to tie that knot and hang on through the swing of emotions. Then use that same knot to take the next step upward. Don't get stuck in the web of confusion. Do what you know, and let the rest of the web be until you can sort through it to a better understanding. With every hurdle jumped, it is one more level of healing reached and a milestone to be placed in this triumph over brokenness.

6. Embrace your brokenness

There was a situation in my youth that could have turned out ugly. I was enjoying a summer day with a relative and a friend, and we headed to the local creek. I am not a swimmer by any means. I am a sinker and a heavyweight. I have a great respect for the water. Anyhow, on this summer day, I was splashing around in the water fully suited up with a life jacket. If it got too deep and began to lift my feet from the bottom, I hurriedly made my way to shallower water. I watched as my other two friends grabbed the rope that was tied to the underside of the bridge and would swing out and jump off into a pretty deep hole. It looked fun, but I was not going to be giving in to their persuasion to join them in this swing, jump routine. I cannot really tell you what happened other than I waded a bit too close to the deep spot and slipped off the hidden edge. I was immediately a human buoy. I panicked! My life preserver came loose and was no longer preserving, and I began to sink. I was drinking way too much water, and in between the bobbing, I was gasping, yelling, and sucking some more water. My friends rushed to my rescue, but I began to fight them. I began to pull them under with my sinking episodes. Finally, I was able to let go, and I allowed their expertise to lead me to safety. I embraced the help.

Embracing the brokenness is simply to recognize it is there and accept it. Don't fight its existence because it will only prolong the recovery and hurt others in the process. Embracing your brokenness is not at all suggesting you develop the victim mentality; it's just the opposite. You accept it by not denying its presence, and you in turn also accept the help being given to overcome the effects of your brokenness. This embrace of your situational brokenness helps to lift the oppressiveness often associated with the pain of your traumatic experience.

I can affirm to you this embrace is life altering. It might be humbling, but it was so liberating at the same time. I did not need to perform any longer. I found a new identity in spite of the scars and struggles I had. I could happily embrace life and look into my tomorrows without wondering if I was ever going to be accepted again. I am still learning the process of altering my learned negativity. Yes, I know it is part of my broken story, but it's changed and is still being changed by His grace. I have fallen in love with the person of Jesus. He is making me brand-new in Him.

7. Find your new normal

This may be one of the most challenging steps to implement. It's natural to resist change, but our traumatic experiences brought you change without you inviting it. Now we have to make necessary adjustments. You never thought about being alone, but it's a new reality. Death, divorce, separations, or relocations usher us quickly into a whole new phase of life. You do not need to end living because your personal environment was drastically altered. Don't be rash or hastily try to fix it, but grieve the loss, adjust your focus, and take what steps you can or need to reacclimate back into a whole new dimension of life. Even after you start to function, there will be continual aspects of change and adjustment. It's normal. Emotional challenges will occur. Your coping mechanisms will be stretched and maybe break. Your world may have been turned upside down, but it doesn't need to stay that way. Your life was severely altered, but life continues and you can find a new purpose and meaning to exist. You may have been used to being a follower and now you need to lead. Don't try leading from your head, but lead from your heart. Put God in charge and allow Him to direct your steps. "*Trust in the Lord with all your heart, and do not lean on your own understanding. In all your ways acknowledge Him, and He will make straight your paths*" (Pr. 3:5–6 ESV). Putting your faith and trust in God may be your new normal, but it is the best new normal you could ever experience. God truly knows what He is doing.

I cannot tell you what your picture of wholeness will look like. I cannot promise there will never be another traumatic experience or another revelation of brokenness. What I can tell you is that there is a way up and a way to overcome all those crisis moments. There even might be some lingering side effects of those experiences of brokenness, but I assure you that hope is found when you look to God and place your surrendered life into His hands.

***Don't try leading from your head,
but lead from your heart***

Misconceptions of the Recovery Process

It's over, why isn't it erased?

Just because you processed a traumatic experience does not necessarily mean you are "over it." What does it really mean to be recovered? What does recovery look like? Recovering from the bottom of brokenness is a process. It is a strengthening of your emotional stamina. It is the development of healthier coping mechanisms. It is the retraining of your mind which definitely is an ongoing exercise. To think you have accomplished a permanent triumph is to set yourself up for disappointment. Every victory is a stepping stone to the next revelation of something broken or needing to be overcome. In fact, a step forward may lead to a couple of steps in the opposite direction. We don't like reverses, but sometimes the reverse gear is necessary, so you can move forward more efficiently, just in a better direction. I don't want to paint a picture that brokenness is a constant headache or battle because it isn't. There is a place of sweet release and a restful peace. I am, however, endeavoring to present a caution, so that an improper opinion or elation of triumph is not misguided to a false sense of completion.

Has the devil ever went digging in the boneyard of your past? Yes, they are covered by the blood and forgiveness from Christ was received. Satan doesn't care about all of that, he just wants to remind us of our yesterdays, and he keeps throwing negative after negative feeling and impression into our minds. He increases the intensity and slams some hurtful accusations against us. Being accused is never easy to digest, but when the accusations are many and on a continual basis, what should one assume? It may be easy for some to reply just resist and he will flee. Absolutely. I agree, but when the accusations are coupled with the scars of a traumatic experience, it creates a battlefield of the mind. Even though one might have worked through all the baggage of the crisis, its memory spawns all kinds of questions as to the validity of triumph he or she was sure to have occurred.

The pathway of forgiveness does not mean the erasing of our memory. There are some traumatic experiences that will never be erased. The pain is too real and raw, and the scars are too deep. Unfortunately, two words have been combined that have left victims of trauma struggling in their grief. These two words are *forgive* and *forget*. It slips from off our tongues as the true prescription of healing, but it is not accurate at all if you do not define your terms. For most, those two words hold different meaning and are impossible to combine as the script for recovery. For one, they are not totally accurate by scripture in application to our human limitations. What is God's choice to not remember against us does not mean our minds can simply erase our traumatic experiences. What is possible is the coping procedure when our mind wants to continue recalling this negativity.

Trigger points and flashbacks

Alongside our highways and country roads are miniature memorials where a life was tragically lost. I have seen some elaborate memorials. Is this helpful or is it hurtful? Does it bring any type of closure to the family and friends who are trying to process their grief?

It may seem like it is expressing an honor upon the deceased, but it is actually reinforcing the traumatic event.

I am not the only person who has injured themselves by a deep scratch or cut. In the healing process, a scab is formed as the exposed flesh and skin regains a new closure for the wound. What happens when you pick at the scab? It opens the wound again, exposing the wound to a raw condition. The continual picking at the scab increases the likelihood of a permanent scar and, for sure, an extended time for healing. These roadside crosses are like picking the scab off our wounds. The daily commutes to work, school, or the store are constant reminders of our pain and loss. This constant visual stimulation is re-inflicting the wounds and the whole process of adjustments following this tragedy. It is taking the grieving process and throwing it in reverse. There needs to be a decisive point of taking down these roadside memorials and leaving our moments of reflection and grief for the cemetery.

I love fireworks. The bigger, the better, and the more those sonic booms rumble the chest, the more pleasure I find. I am patriotic and I am proud to be an American. So on holidays that celebrate our American heritage, I will celebrate with patriotic tradition. I do not appreciate the moral direction America is going, but when our military power is displayed, I am all engaged. I am honored to be a proud parent of two US Marines. However, there are those who struggle, not because they are not a patriotic American, but the sounds take them back to a battlefield and the horrors of war. Images of their dead comrades play like a cinematic movie, but it's real life for them. The rhythmic pulse of gunfire echo in their heads, causing a ringing of the ears for many days. These flashback encounters are troublesome and create moments of panic for the one trying to overcome this internal brokenness that inhibits their daily routines of life. Anyone who has had a traumatic experience probably will have flashbacks. The goal in this recovering process is to have less occurrences and a better way of responding when they do happen.

Trigger points are those events that tip the scales, causing one to revisit the accumulation of crisis events stored internally. The interesting fact is the trigger point may have nothing to do with a particular current situation. This happens to many first responders. The services, of first responders of all professions, are called upon not because it is a happy occasion, but a desperate critical emergency. Training allows them to keep engaged, but there will be a tipping point when they can no longer hold another critical incident without processing all the details and emotions that have been stored for a long time. These triggers are like an internal explosion of emotion. They see a sight, smell a certain odor, or make unique correlations between current details and something from the past. The stress button was triggered, and there is necessity to talk and work through it immediately. For many, they declare they are okay. There is too much stigma to ask for help or to talk with someone. The numbers are increasing, but too many walk away, never to engage in emergency services again. Some can no longer cope and choose suicide. There currently is a crisis in numbers both in the rise of suicides, but also the vacancy of replacements or shuttered doors of emergency service agencies.

The encounter of flashbacks or other trigger points does not mean you are incomplete or permanently broken. You are human. Overcoming any element of brokenness is not the elimination of any memory or the revisiting of its reality. Overcoming is the healthy response to these flashbacks and trigger points. You do not need to get hung up for an extended length of time. You move through it and beyond it, enabling a return to your current normal activity.

The stigma of weakness

Why is it okay to go the doctor for our aches and pains, and yet it is not okay to find help for emotional pain? Why is it legitimate to ask the mechanic to diagnose the grinding and other obscene noises of our vehicles, and somehow it is not valid to seek help to diagnose our internal struggles to process our trauma? *"Pride goes before destruction, and a haughty spirit before a fall"* (Pr. 16:18 NKJV). There is nothing weak about asking for help. It is more indicative of strength and confidence than an inferior perception of weakness. The unfortunate stigma associated with various kinds of interventions has led too many to self-destruct. Procrastination does not work for your benefit either. Remember that knocking sound from the motor in your car? Well, you should have checked your oil level, but because you put it off, you have now ceased up your engine and it is no longer operable. What could have been a few dollars for a quart or two of oil is now a major expense to replace the motor and the labor to get the job complete. Therapeutic intervention is so much better than a neurological breakdown.

The nostalgic position of "I'm okay" is not always accurate. Fear of the alternative keeps us claiming the cliché "I'm fine." If this is an accurate truth, by all means, don't change. But if it may not be completely accurate, by all means, reach out for help. Get beyond the macho, hero complex and speak to someone about your internal wrestling. Many times, it's the other people in our life who realize there is some problem. Family and friends are a good barometer for our outburst and sour dispositions. Not all ailments can be visually seen, but we know the symptoms. Symptoms of stress responses are telltale signs that something isn't right. A listing of the symptoms of stress is discussed in discovering your self-care plan. Face your fear of being stereotyped and reach for outside help, so you can work through your past and find the internal strength to overcome.

It is okay to depend on God for everything.

Someone said that it's a sign of weakness to be dependent upon Christ for everything. I am okay with this false diagnosis. Christ is so much stronger than I am. He knows so much more than I do. He for sure has my best interest always in mind. So yes, I trust Him for everything, and it is on His strength I depend. The Apostle Paul requested from God to remove a "thorn" in his flesh. God said no, but He added why. *"My grace is sufficient for you, for my power is made perfect in weakness"* (2 Cor. 12:9 ESV). Listen to the response. *"Therefore, I will boast all the more gladly of my weakness, so that the power of Christ may rest upon me"* (2 Cor. 12:9 ESV). This is a healthy response to what is broken. It is okay to depend on God for everything.

Safety in Self-Care

It was a subliminal message, but in my early years of learning, retaining knowledge, and life experiences, it was "spiritual" to burn out for Jesus. I heard one precious lady tell me that a Christian cannot burn out. I politely disagree, but it is this hidden message that troubles me. For those in ministry, how is it God-honoring to burn the candle at both ends busying yourself with ministry obligations, spend late nights in the office, up early to rush off to somewhere, and to be everything for everyone else and yet be justified in your mind because it is the Lord's work? Wow…I'm exhausted just writing that sentence. Is it okay to wear yourself out and sacrifice your family in the process? Where is your ministry priorities, and who is at the top of the list? It was in my firefighter training and emergency medical training that this phrase, "take care of yourself" was often used. "Is the scene safe?" is the first question to ask. Why? If your rush into a fire or medical emergency without stopping to consider your own safety, you can very easily be another casualty. So instead of one victim, there now are two or more because you did not think about your own self. It is not selfish to think about self-care.

Self-care is the preventative maintenance of our triumph over brokenness. It is crucial to establish a self-care plan, so there is not a regress into debilitating functionality. I cannot say exactly what that plan looks like for you. You have to set up these steps in accordance to your personal likes and workability. It will take decisive decision to maintain. It will necessitate your commitment and time. It will not happen on its own. It takes your involvement to establish, so you can reap the benefit. I offer ingredients that need to be a part of any self-care plan you implement. Make it profitable and enjoyable.

1. Keep in contact with God.

Knowing God is a personal relationship. It is imperative to have daily devotions with Him. You have to set up your boundaries, so nothing comes between you and Him. What are daily devotions? It is a deliberate time to make contact with God. Devotions include: reading the Bible, praying, and time for quiet meditation. Reading the Bible needs to be a daily routine; its content are the principles for godly living. Find devotional readings to add to your time in the Word. Prayer is a spoken language of devotion and worship. Worship while you pray. Be confident in your requests for His outpoured grace and intervention. Make sure you say thank you to Him. It's God's prescription, not mine. Meditating is when we become still. Listen for His responses to our praying and worship. *"Meditate within your heart on your bed, and be still." "Be still, and know that I am God"* (Ps 4:4, 46:10 NKJV).

2. Keep connected where God is.

This principle supports our daily devotions. Where can I find God in the routines of life? For one, God tells us to get to church. This is your faith family. They are your support group. They will be your closest friends, even your confidants. *"Not forsaking the assembling of ourselves together"* (Heb. 10:25 NKJV). Jesus set a good example of going to the synagogue. If He went to church, so should we. There are various ways to keep connected with others, especially for the strengthening of faith. There are opportunities of gospel concerts, fellowship meals, and Bible studies that provide opportunity to keep this connection from becoming a disconnection.

3. Be careful in our choices

Be sensitive to God and His Holy Spirit in how you conduct your lifestyle. Do nothing that would grieve Him (Eph. 4:30). Put nothing before you that associates you with evil rather than that which speaks of Christ. Habits of our lives are not innocent benign details. The places we go and the things we might participate in can shipwreck our course of action in our recovery of brokenness. Spirituality isn't automatic; you have to pursue after godly living. When you have experienced a traumatic incident that produces a form of brokenness, your coping mechanisms need to be supportive of your faith in God.

4. Follow your therapeutic plan

Talk with your Pastor. I suggest you start with him, and maybe he can offer the referral for outside help. A true pastoral shepherd will be supportive of you finding other means of help to discuss issues that are not directly connected with the subject of faith. I would most of all recommend finding a Christian counselor. Their premise of their therapeutic intervention coincides with the principle of faith. Christ is primary; all else is secondary, but supportive of the primary. Fact…we do not like to be uncomfortable. Most often, we shun or shy away from what disrupts that feeling. When a therapist is helping to process your experiences of life, follow through with the process. Yes, it might be uncomfortable at times, but it is necessary to overcome what has plagued you for too long. Follow the steps, do their recommendations, and keep your appointments.

5. Recognize stress and destress

Stress is harmful in so many applications. Stress compounds our problems. Our situations raise our stress levels, and we need to be aware of the whole connection of the details of our brokenness and the levels of stress. Consider these common signs and signals of stress reaction:

Physical: fatigue, nausea, twitches, chest pain, rapid heart rate, headaches, elevation of blood pressures, hair loss, chills or profuse sweating.

Cognitive: confusion, blaming others, poor attention, poor decisions, memory problems, nightmares, hypervigilance, intrusive images, difficulty calculating or identifying objects.

Emotional: anxiety, guilt, grief, denial, panic feelings/attacks, emotional shock, depression, irritability, agitation, loss of emotional control, intense anger, obsessiveness.

Behavioral: change in speech, withdrawal, emotional outbursts, suspiciousness, loss or increase of appetites, inability to rest, pacing, ritualistic behavior, virtually anything out of normalcy.

Spiritual: questioning faith, self-blame, questioning God, anger at God, realization of mortality, withdrawal from faith and religious practices, questions about good and evil, redefining moral value, concern vengeance, questions about forgiveness.

We have, naturally as well as deliberately, done things to destress. We may have a hobby, or go to the woods for a hunt. Some have found walking with a pet helps to deescalate from stress. I had some pets who raised my stress levels. Stress is disruptive just like our brokenness. Our normal routines are cancelled out. We sit in a daydream stare not sure where to go or what to do next.

Here are some very important things to keep doing regularly:
Get as much sleep as possible.
Eat healthy food.
Keep exercising.
Drink plenty of water.
Keep connected with family and friends.
Here are some things not to do:
Don't make any major decisions—life changing decisions.
Don't resist the feelings, flashbacks, or bad dreams.

Don't break your normal routines.

If you are observing these signs of stress in others, listen with an open heart and mind to your friends and family. They have a story to tell. Do not take any outbursts personally. Give adequate space, but do not allow them to be alone.

6. Establish a self-care plan

Your self-care plan needs to have scheduled time off and space to vacation. Vacations are the break from the daily grind with a different focus which provides a healthy reboot to emotional and cognitive coping mechanisms.

My childhood was good. I can't say it was exceptional, but I have no complaints. However, I never remember going on a vacation with my parents and siblings. Now there are pictures to prove there were vacations, but by the time I entered the world, time and money did not allow it. When I became a married man and then a father, together as a family, we made it a point to take vacations. Only a couple of times were they rather expensive adventures, but mostly they were times to be together enjoying the outdoors and away from the hubbub and busyness of life. As a family, we have some serious cherished memories of vacations. They are the best medicine to take, and they need to be an important part of your self-care plan.

I never heard of self-care in the beginning of my ministry years. I am not sure I ever had a class about developing a self-care plan in my undergraduate studies. It may have been mentioned in passing, but never discussed in detail. For me, anything involving self was a negative and did not reflect spirituality. Selfishness is anti-Christ, but self-care is not about an absorbance of self, but a healthy love for yourself to take care of yourself. Health and wholeness need to have self-care.

It is not selfish to think about self-care.

Let me explain why this self-care plan is so important now in my life. I grew up learning how to work at a very young age. Truthfully, too young, when I consider the intensity of how it was presented. It developed into a pattern of intensity, so much so that I did not learn how to have fun. There were occasions of fun-filled pleasures, but intensity became a driving force in my work ethic. I worked hard and long. I remained busy doing something. I did not sit around. There was too much to do to sit and do nothing. I sacrificed the time I should have spent with my wife and boys and condoned my actions because I was active in ministry. You can be too busy in ministry if you neglect your family by not providing the needed leadership roles God has laid on husbands and fathers. God was aware of my drive, and so He put a circuit breaker in my body that trips when overload has been going for too long. God put me down in bed with the most intense migraine that made me very nauseous and the hater of any kind of light.

I would be overwhelmed with guilt feelings if I sat down or spent some hours doing virtually nothing. In the process of God breaking me down and showing me the truth about myself, I came fully aware that this drive is not wholesome. It was destroying my boys inwardly, and it built some wedges into some of my parishioners of my early ministry. The faithfulness of God showed me and taught me, through His Word, that there is a purpose to Jesus slipping away from the crowd. The truth he told to the disciples to come aside and find rest was not a suggestion, but a principle. The importance of the Sabbath day was not just a day to direct our attention toward God, but it also says that we are to cease from all our work…and rest. This is exactly what the Creator did. I needed to follow His example. What a difference it makes in all areas of life when you stay true to biblical principles and practice those principles in your daily life.

So now, not so pleasant conversation. I have had some self-destructive behavior. I already mentioned early about my negative thought processing, but this self-destructive behavior is my physical health. I love food and enjoy food. My all-time favorite is a good juicy burger done on the charcoal grill with a fresh garden tomato, lettuce, and onion topped with a spread of miracle whip and a squirt of ketchup. When I was young, I never had a problem with weight. In fact, pictures show I was almost too thin. Remember my traumatic experience of my first funeral of the twenty-one-year-old accident victim? Something broke inwardly to my physical composition, and it appears it has become evident in my physical weight. It was following that traumatic event that I began to steadily gain weight. I jokingly blamed my wife I put on sympathy weight when she was pregnant with our firstborn son. I did gain quite a bit during those months, but it had nothing to do with her. For years, I never really linked weight gain to my traumatic experience. It was after the fact that I began to realize of a potential correlation.

My weight is a personal challenge for me. I do believe that deliberate obesity does not honor God, nor bring glory to Him. Eating habits that violate principles of temperance and border on gluttony speak more of sin than of innocence. I am not diagnosing your weight situation and blaming you of anything. I know some dear friends who have a physiological issue that make weight a situation beyond their ability to control. Let's be gracious in our judgements and opinions. I am referencing myself only. I am making no excuses—just being honest.

I have done diets in different ways. Cardiac diets, low carb diets, low calorie diets, etc. are just a few samplings of my endeavors. I have done dieting along with some exercise, and it has helped. I have hit the proverbial plateau at different times and cannot seem to go beyond a certain point. I lose and then I gain; the cycle continues. I have had different illnesses that were good jump-starts to losing weight, but the challenge continues. My sweet, lovely wife has tried to keep after me to keep engaged in this process of weight loss. Does weight loss take discipline? Absolutely! Do I have discipline? Not as strict as I need to. For sure, my weight loss journey is quite a winding path with some downhill runs but many uphill battles. I need to lose weight, and I am trying to lose weight, but weight loss is a huge hurdle. It's a mind battle that plays out in my eating habits. I am daily aware of this struggle. So what do I do to face this hurdle? I keep trying and keep working at this real challenge in my life. I do not want to speak negatively of Christ through the immensity of my size. Thin is no guarantee of spiritual stature, but neither is greatness in size. So the journey continues. My self-care plan does include the subject of food and eating habits. What's in your plan to promote health and wholeness for all dimensions of your life?

It may be beneficial to include some accountability individuals to help you in this process of self-care planning. It may be your husband or wife as well as your children. Children are not as naive as we too often assume. They can sense and tell when things are out of balance. They can be our check and balance to maintain a proper stress level and to keep our self-care plans in place. What good is a self-care plan if it is not integrated into our lives? Plan it and then do it. It could save you from additional problems and crisis experiences if you take the time to take care of yourself.

Celebrate Your Triumphs

The darkness that envelops our lives from the brokenness inside us births seeds of doubt and hopelessness. It presents itself as doom and gloom. If we allow these seeds of negativity to take root, it will bring us to an even darker place of the soul. The flood of negative thoughts upon our minds seems to block any ray of hope; we are left feeling hopeless. Where can one find a new beginning? Where do you look? Obviously, the picture within us can be a dark negative. We have to look beyond ourselves. There is a stunning picture just waiting to be developed. There is hope and help if we look upward to God and focus upon the correct truths.

I lay across the seats in my school bus in literal pain. My gut hurt, and my stomach was quite nauseous. I was groaning in prayer, and puddles of tears dotted the bus floor. In my anguish, a tender whisper came to my ear, "Look up." I was. I was staring at the bus ceiling. "No, look beyond what your eyes can see and look at me." It was in this moment that Psalm 121 birthed a message of hope. My travail was trying to think of what to say to a distraught community over an untimely death. I had to get beyond myself and see the true source of help. *"My help comes from the Lord, who made heaven and earth"* (Ps. 121:2 ESV). The whole Psalm was a powerful encounter with an Omnipotent God. He came into the bus and ministered directly to my soul. He strengthened me in my hour of brokenness and weakness and lifted me up to Himself. I still had to face the responsibility of speaking hope to these hurting people, but I was not alone. I could celebrate the presence of God empowering my internally.

We have to celebrate every triumph, every victory, every measure of help, every dose of encouragement because it is internal fuel to overcome the oppressive nature of brokenness. Celebration can put on many different faces. You need to speak this celebration. Publicly testify in praise to God. Make His praise known in the sanctuary of His people. Offer the sacrifice of praise. Tell someone in person on purpose. For every believer, we need to be celebrating Jesus. The story of our triumph is not about me or you; it is all about Him. We need to make the most about Jesus. The exaltation of Christ should be our normal conversation. It is God, our Heavenly Father, Jesus Christ, our Living Redeemer, the Holy Spirit, our Faithful Comforter, together, that have given us a living Hope. It is hope that keeps our journey to wholeness progressing. As you tell your triumphs, it reinforces this victory into our thought processes. These triumphant victories are stored antidotes, so when the uprisings from our brokenness take us backward, we remember and recall our victories. It brings this slide backward to a halt.

All depends on the degree of triumph; you might need to celebrate at a separate location. It can be a simple dining out experience, or a picnic lunch at the park or alongside the creek. Make it a pleasurable occasion, so it also reinforces your victory. Don't be too expensive or elaborate; keep it relevant to your story. Your celebration needs to be complimentary so that your triumph becomes a distraction in the recovery process instead of focusing on the pain or hurt of your brokenness. Take someone else with you on these celebratory outings. Your immediate family is an excellent place to begin. Remember, your journey has also been a part of their own life's story. Don't exclude them, but include them. What an excellent way to celebrate a victory, but by doing it with your family, it's also in keeping of a necessary aspect of your self-care plan. These activities together can even provide a nice element of exercise. Be creative; it's inspirational!

Write down your stories of triumph. Keep a logbook, diary, or journal. Once it is written, it now becomes a reference resource when discouragements happen. Be prepared, discouragements will always be there, but so will the stories of your triumphs. They are messages of encouragement. Books have been written from the compilation of stories from a journey of victory.

Celebration is not a sullen, downcast countenance. It's a smile and probably a little bit of noise. I have never been to a sporting event where celebration was done quietly. Every point earned was reason to celebrate. Think about this celebration. *"There is joy in the presence of the angels of God over one sinner who repents"* (Luke 15:10 NKJV). We need to celebrate every time there is a victory over sin. We need to make some noise over every triumph of brokenness that has been accomplished. It doesn't matter how big or how small… *celebrate*!

We need to make the most about Jesus. The exaltation of Christ should be our normal conversation. It is God, our Heavenly Father, Jesus Christ, our Living Redeemer, the Holy Spirit, our Faithful Comforter, together, that have given us a living Hope.

Keep Hope Alive

In an era where there is so much negative news and public expressions of hurt, pain, and sorrow, we have to keep the right focus so that our hope remains vibrant. Hope is not just a positive outlook on life. Being positive helps, but it's not hope. Hope has to be born within. Hope is a fruit of a life found in God. Hope is birthed when there is a spiritual new birth in Christ. Outside of Christ, you have no hope that will last. The hope found in Jesus Christ is an eternal hope that does not fade away.

This eternal hope is founded in our eternal home of heaven. With heaven as our goal, this is where we lay up our treasures and live with an eternal perspective about all of life's situations. Decisions we make, expenditures of finances, choices of soul mates or careers all combined—we consider His direction and leading. We build upon the talents that God Almighty has gifted, and we do all for the glory of God.

I have heard many people who have faced near-death experiences, including myself—it has a way of putting everything into a different perspective. We get caught up in the demands of work, home, and even church, that we lose sight of a greater picture that is more important. We take nothing with us that is tangible. We take our soul alone, and our eternal soul must know of the wholeness that is found in Jesus Christ. Wholeness brings hope—a bright hope for our tomorrows.

> Therefore, since we are surrounded by so great a cloud of witnesses, let us also lay aside every weight, and sin which clings so closely and let us run with endurance the race that is set before us, looking to Jesus, the founder and perfecter of our faith, who for the joy that was ser before him, endured the cross, despising the shame, and is seated at the right hand of the throne of God. (Heb. 12:1–2 ESV)

Don't dismiss your hope when a setback may occur in your journey of healing. Life will still present challenges, and there will still be tests, trials, and other temptations until our time on earth has been completed. God knows you, and He is fully aware of every detail in your life. Call out to Him, and I am confident that He will sustain you. *"The eternal God is your refuge, and underneath are the everlasting arms"* (Deut. 33:27 NKJV). Those strong arms will not grow weak and let you fall. They are all-powerful. Rest in the arms of God and be comforted in Him. He is your everlasting Hope.

Epilogue

The Journey Continues…

God directed my path for a period away from full-time ministry. I was deeply emotionally broken and was nowhere fit to minister to others. I became a good parishioner and supported my pastor in any way possible. It was good for me to occupy a pew for a while. It was during this sabbatical period that I slipped behind the wheel of an eighteen-wheeler and did some trucking. I actually had my family with me on a small extended trip when the call came that my father was taken to the hospital. He had been hospitalized already for two weeks and was sent home. There was a return of symptoms and was admitted once again.

It was discovered during this second admittance that he had substantial blood clots. I told my family I would be home as soon as I could, but I was out of state with my job. I was finishing up at a graduation ceremony and celebration when my phone rang again, and the news was that something seriously happened to dad and I needed to get home quickly. I rushed through the day and into the night to get back, and early the next morning, my family and I made it to the hospital to see my father. I was a bit apprehensive as to what I might find, but I stepped around the corner to see my dad sitting up in his bed. His breathing was a bit labored, but he smiled and we embraced. It was the next gesture that took me to my knees. My father took both of my hands and said carefully and passionately that he was not coming out alive. I protested, but I knew he knew something I did not.

The conversation continued. He shared his concern for me, but he also fully understood and supported and encouraged me. I assured him I would be returning to ministry as soon as God opened the door. With my hands still grasped in his, he began to pray a blessing over me and my family. I was moved to the core. I trembled and shook from sobbing so hard. The remembrance of this God-moment still moves me to tears. We sang and worshiped in his hospital room on that Sunday morning. By that afternoon, my whole immediate family was gathered in the hospital, knowing my dad would soon step from earth to his home in heaven. He was on no medications or even oxygen, but the clots had already taken their toll, and his vital organs were shutting down. The next couple of days were a roller coaster of emotions, and he would slip so close and then arouse and yell at us to get home or go to work. On one occasion, he awoke, except he was rejoicing and praising God. He was seeing things and hearing music that only his eyes and ears could comprehend. Every nurse in the hospital stood outside his door as tears were streaming down all of our faces. It was a powerful moment. He then slipped back to sleep.

I didn't want to go to work, but my mother insisted I take a short little run to at least keep a few dollars coming my direction. My dad was a faithful hardworking man. I remember the time I sat with him in the ER following a weird breakout of hives while having our evening family devotions. As they informed him of his need to remain hospitalized for observation, he began to cry. I tried to assure him it was okay and it was a precautionary measure. His tears were not for worry, but of disappointment. He informed me he had never missed a day of work in thirty-three years. This was going to be his first. I was stunned. My admiration for this man, my dad, just increased substantially.

My wife went to her teaching responsibility, and I slid into the truck and headed off. I was just minutes from my delivery destination when my phone rang again. My sister was informing me that again, something major transpired and it was going to be very soon for his passing. I got to my delivery place, but was an emotional train wreck. They hurriedly off-loaded my trailer, and I hastily began my journey back to see my father. I called my wife to give her the update, and she grabbed our boys from school and rushed toward the hospital. She was running, but was met by my sibling in the hall. She relayed my message to give to my dad if I could not make it back in time to do it myself.

My mom leaned down to my dad's ear and said, "Mark is on his way, but he wants you to know that he loves you and he is going to keep preaching." The monitors revealed his attempt at responding, but in a few short seconds he was gone, and he was in the presence of holy angels and his Savior Jesus Christ. I was told of this account by phone, and I had to pull over to the side of the road. My tears were too heavy to see properly. I was broken in sorrow, and yet I was rejoicing in hope. It was the hope of faith that was to carry me through and still carries my reliant heart and soul.

God put me to the test of keeping my word because it was only two days following his passing that I received another call, except this one was the offer to become a candidate for a Senior Pastoral position. I affirmed I could come—not this immediate Sunday because I was preaching my father's funeral—but the following Sunday I would. Even from the moment the call came, it felt right and it felt uplifting. It was just a few days following that Sunday of my trial message that the call came they had unanimously voted for me to come be their Pastor. I accepted over the phone and now, many years later, I am still filling that position as their pastor and will do so until God leads otherwise. God has worked mightily in my behalf, and I am thankful.

God is an amazing God, and He is not defined or limited to the brokenness that may be on the inside of man.

There is nothing special about me in this journey; what is special is the grace of God. My story has been interesting to experience and yet an amazing one as I have seen the hand of God at work for me and within me. God is an amazing God, and He is not defined or limited to the brokenness that may be on the inside of man. He is a supernatural abundant life giver that pours into us a healing that inspires us and changes us from simply performing a duty to now sharing because of a depth of compassion. This compassion could only be realized because of the brokenness God allowed to be, so I could understand the brokenness that Christ came to heal. In Christ this is hope; there is wholeness. I know it personally to be true, and you can enjoy it too. In my brokenness, God was my strength. Jesus is the healer of the brokenhearted.

Never forget, God is still writing your story. When He is the Author, you simply follow His lead. There will always be lessons to learn, valleys to walk, and mountains to climb. Clouds may form or the sun will shine brightly, yet whatever season is present, being as close to Jesus as possible is where you are the safest. *"Yea, though I walk through the valley of the shadow of death, I will fear no evil; For you are with me, Your rod and staff, they comfort me"* (Ps. 23:4 NKJV). In the center of His will is being right next to Jesus; you will never go wrong with Him. The safest place to be is next to Him in the center of His will. Don't close the book because you don't like the story. God has a greater plan and purpose beyond you that He wants to fulfill, and you could be the link for someone to find Him. Revel in being the vessel or channel He is using for His glory. Your brokenness can be your testimony of God's grace, intervening in your behalf even though you might struggle with the process.

On which side of brokenness are you? Are you stuck in your trauma, or are you journeying in triumph? When you let go of your brokenness into the hands of a loving Heavenly Father, there is glorious victory. It is when we hold onto our brokenness and try to solve it ourselves that our journey through life gets messy. Give it to Jesus—He is the perfect load carrier.

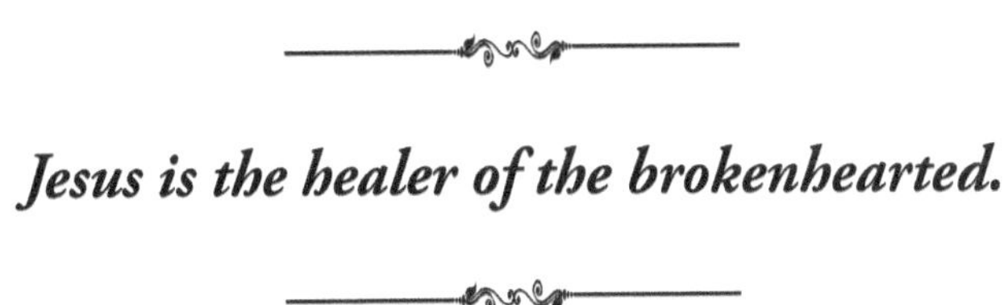

Jesus is the healer of the brokenhearted.

Resources

These are potential resources and tools in coping with brokenness and the helps in finding a God who cares. I recommend these books because I have found some tremendous help within their pages.

1. The Holy Bible—God; Highly Recommend
2. *Why You do the Things You Do* by Dr. Tim Clinton and Dr. Gary Sibcy
3. *Wounds That Heal* by Stephen Seamands
4. *Your Scars are Beautiful to God* by Sharon Jaynes
5. *Healing for Damaged Emotions* by David Seamands
6. *Healing of Memories* by David Seamands
7. *Freedom from the Performance Trap* by David Seamands
8. *Grace* by Max Lucado
9. *What's So Amazing about Grace?* by Philip Yancy
10. *Help for the Fractured Soul* by Candyce Roberts

For music to be the right kind of help, it needs to describe your heart, soul, and mind, but it also needs to direct your attention to God. This kind of music has healthy, healing qualities.

About the Author

Mark Fultz is an ordained minister and has been in ministry for well over thirty years. The majority of those years have been in Pastoral Ministry. He holds a bachelors in ministerial studies and a master of arts in pastoral care and counseling. He married his high school sweetheart, and God has blessed them with three beautiful children, two lovely daughters-in-law, and two precious grandchildren. Mark, along with his family, has shared his love for God through music and evangelistic endeavors across the Midwest and Eastern US while his Pastoral Ministry has allowed him to reside in his home state of Pennsylvania.

Mark's ministry has allowed him to be a licensed and credentialed as an EMR, a firefighter, and a FF Chaplain. He is a leader in crisis intervention as mental health and peer support for all first responders. His ministry experiences are many, but it is Mark's love for God and his compassion for people that accurately defines his speaking ministry as effective and inspirational. As a published author, his ministry expands beyond the pulpit or the private setting in counseling to include the printed page—a resource in providing guidance to any who may struggle with asking for help but will read.

May God be glorified, and the name of Jesus exalted.